There Must Be an Ocean
Betv

· To Shoshana Cardin
Thanks for helping
me tell the story of
One of the "1000 children"
of 1934 ———

Thea K. Lindauer

· Jan 25 · 2009 ·

There Must Be an Ocean Between Us

✦

Letters of Separation and Survival

Letters and their consequences by Samuel Kahn, father of one of the thousand children brought from Germany to the United States in 1934 for an experiment in education.

Thea K. Lindauer

iUniverse, Inc.
New York Lincoln Shanghai

There Must Be an Ocean Between Us
Letters of Separation and Survival

iUniverse books may be ordered through booksellers or by contacting:

iUniverse
2021 Pine Lake Road, Suite 100
Lincoln, NE 68512
www.iuniverse.com
1-800-Authors (1-800-288-4677)

Because of the dynamic nature of the Internet, any Web addresses or links contained in this book may have changed since publication and may no longer be valid.

The views expressed in this work are solely those of the author and do not necessarily reflect the views of the publisher, and the publisher hereby disclaims any responsibility for them.

ISBN: 978-0-595-45240-8 (pbk)
ISBN: 978-0-595-69468-6 (cloth)
ISBN: 978-0-595-89551-9 (ebk)

Printed in the United States of America

This book is dedicated to the wonderful and generous people who created my past, to those who guide my present, and those who are my legacy to the future.

My special thanks go to those who enabled me to set it all down, compelling me to relive it in some instances, and feel the anxieties, the traumas and the spirit of survival—things I was largely unaware of while these events were happening. These giving and gracious people include my three "families:" the Sonnenscheins, the Perlsteins, and my own family, the Kahns of Eisenberg, Germany.

And I could not have dealt with this book without my greatest backer and fan (of more than sixty years), my beloved husband, Harry Lindauer, Colonel, United States Army (Retired). Regretably, he is no longer with us and cannot view—with enormous pride, I am sure—what he so materially helped to create with his love and guidance.

Thea Kahn—11 Years Old

Ich bin gluecklich,
  und wenn ich es nicht bin,
So weiss ich doch das Freud und Leid
  in einer Seele wohnen.

Wolfgang Goethe

I am content,
  And if I'm not,
I know that joy and sorrow
  Live together within my soul.

These have been my guide words for all my growing years,

... and still are.

Thea (Kahn) Lindauer
Annapolis, MD

Contents

Acknowledgements

A book like this cannot be written without the assistance, encouragement, and labor of many different people. I'd like to express my special gratitude to all those who urged me to write it: Professors Gerhardt Sonnert, Larry Thompson, and Joseph Nuesse; to Wilfred Bunge; and to Iris Posner, the Director of The 1000 Children, Inc.

I have nothing but sincere thanks to my good friends and kindred spirits Betty Jane Lindsey, Jane Bailey, and Jim Victor. And last, but certainly not least, my love and thanks go out to my adored family: They have been my perpetual cheerleaders; my all-round noodges and 'gofers'; and have striven mightily to teach me the difference between .jpg, .doc, and .tif, so that this book could actually see the light of day—over electronic means!

Observations

I was almost afraid to reread these letters, much less translate them. So much had happened since then, in the lives of all those concerned, my own in particular. Reading them with the eyes of a 12-year-old who would exclaim, "Thank goodness they're alright!" (*Gott sei Dank, gesundheitlich, Alles geht gut!*) I would then continue with the joyous life of a young girl, being educated in the best way possible.

I realize there are limitations: the family's anxieties, and the censor's watchful eye. Those who look for real political significance will be disappointed. After all, how much of world politics will an anxious father discuss with his 12-year-old daughter an ocean away?

What I can present to you are the feelings that came with these letters in the aftermath of the trauma not experienced the first time around.

This is not your usual Holocaust story of separation, suffering, deprivation and indescribable tragedy. Nevertheless, it too has the reality of separation, fear and uncertainty, even in cared-for circumstances. After the discoveries of the horrors of the Holocaust, there were many guilt feelings about being among the "chosen few." That is what made the obligation to excel much more demanding.

Why me? I was not particularly religious. I did not have the social consciousness that some children possess at a very early age. Still, all these things developed when I became aware of the difference between me and the children in the same privileged strata of society, children who took their enormous privileges so much for granted.

I felt constantly shifted from a pampered child, to one with the weight of the world on her shoulders. Strangely enough, this split in personality did not reflect in my school work.

And so let me begin …

A Family Introduction

Strange ... I can't remember Papa being bombastic, adamantly decisive, or sternly judgmental. I remember a man of slight stature with a twinkle in his hazel brown eyes, a brush of a mustache, a velvety, soothing voice, and a gracious manner. He never punished me. That was always left to Mamma, who ruled the house with a gentle but firm hand. I was never more conscious of this then when egged on by my half-sister Elisabeth, I once challenged Mamma with "I don't have to listen to you, you're only a stepmother!" when she issued some admonition or other. Whoosh!!—The sting of her hand on my rosy rear end echoed throughout the kitchen and the marks were examined in the bathtub nightly for three days. That was the last of my corporeal punishment. Afterwards, for my rebellious behavior I was put into what today is called "time out", or the withholding of some enjoyable treat that I desperately wanted.

Before continuing with the remembrances of my life before I left Germany, I need to clarify some of the intricate relationships that will be prevalent in Papa's letters. I never realized before just how many people came into play. Centered around the core of Papa's and Mamma's relatives, they cross and re-cross through the fact that Papa's first wife was a Lowenstein, sister of Ernest. Mamma, his second wife, was the sister of Lydia, Ernest's wife. So the in-law relationship was doubly enforced.

I cannot speak about the feelings of Frieda Lowenstein when she first saw Samuel Kahn, known as "Solly", a smart young sales representative of a Trier Dry Goods Company. She was a saleslady in a Frankfurt store and, no doubt, showed him in to the owner. In my mind's eye I see a trim figure in a starched white blouse, crisp black skirt and piled up abundant hair in what was then called the "Gibson-girl-look." Somehow, I cannot imagine Papa in a straw hat and bow tie, which was the usual attire for an upcoming young man. I do know it was hard for Jewish young men to meet eligible Jewish young girls, and visa versa. And so a spark was struck. It was not long before he came to call on her, on her weekends off, in Eisenberg in the Palatinate, where her prosperous family lived.

Eisenberg was a growing little metropolis east of Kaiserslautern, in the Pfalz or Palatinate. It was fairly cosmopolitan, having two major industries, surrounded by rural holdings. The main industry was the Von Gienanth Iron Works, owned by the local Baron, who was rarely in residence, but who spent most of his time with the international set in France or Switzerland. The second was the Schiffer and Kirscher Klebsand Werke, a factory that made pipes and conduits of all kinds from a special type of clay found in the area. These two industries drew workers from all along the Rhineland. It was better and cleaner work than mining coal in the Saar Basin. And so with all kinds of municipal services to the worker, plus the surrounding farms, it grew into a little city of some 6,000 people. It served as a transit for the railroad between Kaiserslautern and Ludwigshafen/Mannheim.

Culturally, Eisenberg had the usual festivals, both secular and religious, that were found in most small towns in Germany. In addition, it had classical concerts performed in both Catholic and Protestant churches. It had two Turnhallen (exercise gymnasiums) for movies, plays, and outdoor games. There was a public grammar school through eighth grade and a parochial school run by cloistered nuns. The secondary school (private) in Gruenstadt some 15 miles away started in fifth grade and was reached by railroad. The town had a goodly number of picturesque villas and sturdy townhouses.

This, then, was the town my father visited to court Frieda Lowenstein. After their marriage, he settled there and started his own dry goods business and life insurance agency.

In 1914, Frieda Lowenstein Kahn fell victim to the epidemic Spanish Influenza that was ravaging Europe. Frieda died, and the devastated young father of two little girls left them in the good hands of his loving family, and volunteered as a conscript in the German Army. He was sent to Rumania. After the war ended, he and his comrades literally walked back to Germany, returning in 1919 after everyone had given up hope of finding him alive.

Meanwhile, Frieda Samuel, came to live with her sister Lydia in Eisenberg, and got to know the two little girls who, in turn, became very fond of her. Frieda Samuel came from Alsace-Lorraine and was the daughter of a prosperous bakery owner, Bernard Samuel and his wife Regina, who had eleven children. Fredrika or Frieda Samuel must have been the opposite of the first Frieda. She had bobbed hair and wore loose dresses in modern flapper fashion. She was socially very outgoing and adored by her family. Papa met her on his return from the war in Rumania, courted her, married her, and in 1922, she became my mother. She gave birth to my sister Ruth three years later.

The picture I cherish is one of her in a dress-up mode, her never ending hospitality and romantic attachment to music and the arts. Much of my rearing and that of my sister Ruth was left to a nursemaid named Marie, a very devout Catholic who taught us the Catechism and the Rosary, which we learned along with the Jewish "Sch'ma Israel."

Papa was active in the town council and much respected in the community. With the years, he added a travel agency and Fire Insurance company to his business holdings. Relatives were in abundance around the Palatinate and Alsace-Lorraine and visits back and forth continued all year with vacations and religious holidays spent together. Their lives were those of well-to-do middle-class Germans of mixed religions, socially active with family and neighbors.

There was no particular feeling of being different or alienated from our German neighbors because of our religion. That was to come.

This describes the Samuel Kahn family.

Samuel Kahn, his wife Frieda, and daughter Ruth during a harvest season, 1935.

Prologue

The same World War that took Samuel Kahn from his family for more than two years also deprived the German people of what they perceived as their rightful place in the modern world. Before World War I, German industry, music, and science had been foremost among civilized nations. Losing the War—and, moreover, being punished with economic hardship and a verdict of collective national War Guilt—left the Germans bereft of an identity, and at a loss for an explanation for how the unthinkable could have happened.

When, in 1919, a British officer offhandedly used the expression, "You Germans were stabbed in the back" (reflecting one view that the German military could have continued the fight had it not been for defeatists on the Home Front), a national frenzy to discover, identify, and punish Germany's domestic enemies drove German politics for a decade and a half. Ultra-nationalists blamed the Communists; the Communists blamed the industrialists; the industrialists blamed the Labor unionists. And then there was Adolf Hitler's National Socialist Party, which blamed anyone who seemed a convenient scapegoat. And the most convenient targets were the Jews.

No one has ever completely explained Adolf Hitler's rabid anti-Semitism. Perhaps he was persuaded by the reams of anti-Semitic literature to which he had been exposed in Vienna as an impressionable young man. Nevertheless, he regarded anti-Semitism as the cause of Mankind's ills, and said so in his rambling political treatise, "Mein Kampf" ("My Struggle").

The smug German bourgeoisie took little note of Hitler's hysterical pronouncements. "He's only saying those things to be noticed," they observed. "He doesn't really mean them." But more cautious observers, like Sam Kahn, realized that Hitler—with his seemingly hypnotic gift of oratory—meant every hate-filled word he said.

The year was 1934. Hitler had been in power just over a year …

Papa was a merchant. He dealt in beautiful fabrics, silks from France, woolens from England, and linens from Germany. The front of his store was stocked with all sorts of feminine attire, and the back—for the men—included a tailoring department. Behind it was a windowed office that held all the business ledgers

1

and the important papers for all the agencies he represented: The Hapag and North German Lloyd travel companies; the Münchener and Aachener Fire Insurance Company and the Allgemeine Life Insurance Agency.

For a small town it was a significant business. The house was of brick, large and three-storied, encompassing a wide street-front façade. It contained the store, our living rooms spread over 3 floors, two other three-room flats, and a synagogue. Yes, a synagogue where Papa gathered all the faithful from the entire area for holiday services. Of course, Mamma fed most of them supper during holidays. The right wing contained storage areas and a clay cave, a cold cellar. The back building housed a clothes-washing and drying hall, and a caretaker's room. To the west was a high wall separating us from the neighbor's property. The enclosed courtyard, held one tree, boxes of flowers, and a summer garden house.

Papa frequently went on buying trips. If it was during vacation time, he would take me along. That's how I got to see Humperdinck's opera "Hansel and Gretel" in Frankfurt at Christmastime at the age of five. I began an enchantment with opera which has lasted all my life.

Some years later, early in 1934 Papa came back from one of his Frankfurt trips after I had gone to bed. At breakfast the next morning, he asked me: "How would you like to go on a real journey, a long, long trip, see all of America, and have a wonderful education?" I couldn't contain myself! To see all of these wonders: New York City, the beaches of California, where my half-sister Elsie lived; of course, I would stay away from Chicago, where there were so many shooting gangsters. Yes! Yes! Bright golden visions burst into my head. Mamma kept calmly shushing me: "Listen to Papa".

He went on to explain that while in Frankfurt he had been invited to a meeting where the Hebrew Immigrant Aid Society[1] (HIAS) had a representative speak about sending hundreds of young children from all over Europe (mainly Germany) to the United States to be adopted and integrated into American families and educated to the best of the family's ability. The United States Congress, under the sponsorship of Congresswoman Edith Nourse Rogers, (Rep—Mass) and Senator Robert F. Wagner (Dem—NY), had given its approval. Never was there a mention of escaping a European Holocaust. At that time there was no inkling of such a coming catastrophe. The movement, the Kindertransport", was always referred to as an "Experiment in Education".

Since I could no longer follow the family plan of having me join my older half-sister, Gerda, a medical student in Leipzig, this seemed like a perfect answer.

---

1.   HIAS in "Don't Wave Goodbye" by Phillip K Jason and Iris Posner

My grandfather, still living at the time, asked: "Why can't she go to the relatives in Sweden, or France, or Luxembourg?" I remember Papa standing, cutting the Challah bread and saying very calmly: "There must be an ocean between us."

In the month that followed, Papa was held up to ridicule: Surely he was a heartless monster who didn't care about his young child living among strangers; a doomsayer who didn't know all that Hitler would do for the Jews.

What follows are the letters my father wrote during the three years of our anxiety-filled separation and the vast chasm between our lives.

"There must be an ocean between us."

THE LETTERS

These letters which were written in German are the translated letters and associated concurrent events.

This is an example of an original letter.

1

November 1934

HEADLINES OF THE DAY:

GERMANY—Karl Barth, Leading German Professor, Suspended from University for Refusing to Take Hitler Loyalty Oath

GREAT BRITAIN—Winston Churchill Warns House of Commons of German Air Power

GERMANY—Nazis Order New Music to Replace Jewish Composer Felix Mendelssohn's Score for "A Midsummer Night's Dream"

November 1934

Dear little Thea,

This is the first of what I hope will be a steady stream of wonderful letters between us. We await your first letter most anxiously. Just remember, if writing is at present our only link to you as the telephone calls abroad are so closely monitored—even the most innocent ones are regarded with suspicion.

You looked so eager, so excited, and small waving your goodbyes. I wish I had thought of taking pictures as some of the others did. What awaits you in United States of America, we cannot say. We can only hope that wherever you go, people are awaiting you eagerly and will be kind to you. I have the fullest confidence you will not disappoint them. This is my fervent hope in our shadowy future along with my desire to have you safe.

The card you sent from New York mentions being seasick and in the infirmary all the way across. Please explain. Apparently you were in New York a very short time before you took off for Chicago. You, just as the other six in your shipment, were destined for the Midwest. There are so many questions that we need to have answered, but we know sooner or later, you will put our minds at ease. Mamma and Ruth and I are very sad that you left us, but we all know it's for the very best reason—your education in a free world.

Both your old teacher, Herr Steuer, as well as the new one, Herr Schäfer, hope you will not forget them. They feel very much part of your life, preparing you for a wonderful future in a new land. In today's Germany, for any teacher to feel that way about a Jewish child is rare indeed.

Dear little Thea, I wonder if you know the great responsibility we all have placed on your shoulders. I hope it's not too heavy a burden for you to carry.

Your loving Pappa.

That time in my memory ...

Papa was right. This was the first of a stream of letters that crossed the ocean between us until 1937 when they emigrated. My emotions were very mixed, as they had been ever since we left Eisenberg, amidst tearful goodbyes at the railroad station. My schoolmates and teachers, my sister Gerda, and of course, Papa, who was to accompany me to Hamburg, were gathered around me on that bleak November afternoon. Mamma and Ruth chose to stay at home. At the last moment, as we embraced, Mamma placed a new Shadai (Jewish good luck amulet), around my neck and handed me two letters.

They were from a boy I had met in Erlenbach that last summer vacation, the same boy who had written me at the end of summer. At that time, it was a letter marked "Private", a letter Mamma had made me read to her upon the postman's delivery. I read it with both of them standing there, watching me. After reading it, I tore it up with tears in my eyes, threw it into the fire, and stormed out of the room. I didn't want to do that, but Mamma had made me so angry with what I thought was an intrusion on my privacy. It was a beautiful letter, a poem by Heinrich Heine and reminiscences of a lovely summer for a romantically innocent twelve year old. I never answered it, I wish I had. I remember bursting out of the room crying. Things were never as trusting between Mamma and me again, until now. She sighed as she handed me the new letters with tears in her eyes. I looked at them sadly and tucked them into my handbag. No more words were said. We embraced again, clasping each other tightly, and I was gone.

At the railway station, my friends and teachers waited with a bouquet of red roses. Getting roses in November was quite a tribute, a wonderful compliment. Tears and, sobs were all around us, along with the whispered goodbyes … write … be well … think of us, nothing about what awaited me in the future. This wasn't like going to my aunt's for a summer vacation or a semester away at school. This was going into an uncertain future of a totally new life.

The trip to Hamburg was strangely quiet. My thoughts were all on what was ahead, with hopes of landing on the West Coast in California where my half sister, Elsie, was employed. Once in a while, Papa would come up with some hearty advice such as, writing to everyone, the obligation to my future foster parents, a formidable task; he made references to the landscape we were passing through and touching on the history of Hamburg in general. It was a pity, he said, we had no time to travel through the Elbe Tunnel, an engineering wonder of the time, as it kept traffic flowing under the river, or to see Hummel, the water man, the symbol of Hamburg. Then there was the Hagenbeck Zoo, the largest collection of animals in the world. Normally I would have been very interested, but not that day: My mind was teeming with thoughts about all the many things that were coming into my future.

We stayed at a quiet hotel on the Alster River and since it was dark with a driving rain when we arrived, there was little we could see to distinguish our surroundings.

We had to be at the ship dock at ten AM the next morning to meet our escort and the other children. There were to be seven of us. I, as the youngest, was the only one with parental accompaniment. I don't remember any further significant words of goodbye, only the threefold Biblical blessing with Papa's hands upon my head and the reminder of my responsibilities, nothing—no spoken words about it being possibly the *last time I would see him. He stayed at the dock and I waved and waved until I could see him no longer. If Papa was aware of the fact that I looked so small, I was not conscious of it—I felt like the giant Gulliver; I only sensed the great adventure that lay ahead.*

Thea Kahn (center, wearing a dark dress) and her Seventh Grade classmates

November 1934

Dear Little Thea,

Your first letter from the U.S. arrived at last. What a trip you had crossing the ocean! I saw that the "President Harding" was not the ocean liner you had hoped for but you were well taken care of, particularly in the infirmary. Sitting in a deck chair, watching the sun go down as you sailed out of Queenstown sounds very picturesque and exciting; getting seasick and not being able to get to your cabin is something else. I am glad your cabin-mates finally alerted your escort and the stewardess when they returned and found you absent. It is a pity you had to miss all the on board activities especially getting to know your ship-mates better. Don't be unhappy about it—disappointed, yes, but don't linger on it. Just project ahead to all the other adventures. It must have been quite a shock to awaken on the train in early morning on your way to Chicago and find that the country was so flat. I am sure there are rolling hills and even high mountains in the U.S., just as there are in Europe. You just haven't seen them, yet.

Here, winter is settling in. Christmas preparations are all over town. We are much more aware of Chanukah since you won't be with us, but Mamma and Ruth are sending you their traditional goodies—even chocolate, which is now forbidden to Jews. They now make their chocolate cake out of St. John's (carob) Bread-fruit. For the first time in many years Mamma is not having her tradi-tional "Goose stuffing"—feeding the geese until they are good and fat for Christmas eating. The government has forbidden any Germans to do manual labor for the Jews. Lenchen and her father are allowed to work for us since they live in the house rent free.

We look forward to your next letter about your new home and the nice family who opened it up to you. Your friends send you greetings and want to know if you've seen any Chicago gangsters yet, since that is the picture of Chicago in many European minds.

Your loving Pappa

That time in my memory …

Christmas-time brought a ritual in the family since Grandmother Samuels's time in Alsace-Lorraine. Some women from the town would come nightly and hand-feed a dozen geese, stuffing their open beaks with corn kernels. This was quite a spectacle and it never ceased to fascinate me. The squawking geese, the chattering women and the rattling of the corn buckets made for a raucous and festive atmosphere. The women sat on the long wooden benches holding the geese under their arms, opening their beaks and stuffing in the kernels. The geese grew fat on this nightly ritual. By Christmas, Mamma could use every part of them, except the heads, for some delicacy or other, not to mention the plump soft down pillows that graced every bed, something she learned from her Alsatian mother. It was the highlight of winter activities for all our neighbors.

I remember being quite disappointed that the U.S. Lines "President Harding" was not the "S.S. New York" or "Bremen." But it was a sturdy little passenger/freighter that had been plying the Atlantic Ocean since the early 1920s.

There were only seven of us: Thea Gumpert, Ernst Gutjahr, Alfred Alexander, Hilda Hirsch, Joseph Wechsler, Arnold Bal[1], and myself along with our escort, who were greeted by the captain and the members of the crew, ready to serve us during the voyage. The trip was to take 10 days and we would touch port at Southampton, England, across the channel, at Le Havre, France, and finally dock at Queenstown, Ireland. I was to share a cabin with the other girls, who were fifteen, and would have welcomed a much older shipmate. What made me acceptable was the beautiful wardrobe Mamma had made. I recall a festive dinner with fruit cocktail and banana pudding and whipped cream, which I had never had before. Afterwards, there was a movie, but it was in English, and since I didn't understand it, I went to my cabin. For the first time, I took out the letters Mamma had handed me and opened them holding my breath. Why did Mamma not give them to me before? Only years later, when I had girls of my own, could I understand why she held them back. The fear of losing the precious relationship with the daughter through a new boy and girl encounter seemed so threatening. Nevertheless, the letters which sent my heart pounding were not quite as romantic as I wanted them to be—no poems, only talk of the glorious future of Germany and his role in it. They were very disappointing. That, along with the realization that there was an ocean between me and the family now, dissolved me into tears. I went to sleep resolving to put all of the disheartening European memories behind me.

The next day brought a choppy, bone-chilling crossing to Le Havre, where we took on more cargo and passengers. Then back across the channel to Queenstown, Ireland. Upon leaving that port, the weather cleared for a beautiful sunset, and I stayed on the Promenade deck watching it. I fell asleep in a deck chair and awoke much later in the dark with a most uncomfortable feeling of a heaving stomach. I didn't dare leave my

---

1.   I only learned these names at our recent Chicago symposium when we met with the
     Committee of "The 1000 Children, Inc."

deck chair and crawled miserably under the light steamer blanket, shivering in my too light clothing, hoping someone would come along and find me. After what seemed like hours, someone did and took me to the infirmary, blue and frozen. There the seasickness really took over. By the next morning, now in the throes of a fever and a wheezing cough, it was decided to keep me in the infirmary, which was to be for the remainder of the trip to New York. So much for my glorious adventures on the high seas! All I could see was oceans of tea and soda crackers. Meanwhile, on top of that, I learned what it was to be homesick and long for my family.

New York came up sharp and clear, awesome in appearance. Still weak in my entire body, I did join my shipmates to view the Statue of Liberty, that symbol of welcome to the United States. With all papers and luggage accounted for, we were whisked to an imposing brownstone house in mid-Manhattan. There were more people to welcome us and make sure we were fed and warmly clothed. One thing that sticks in my mind about the house, the dining room and kitchen were below ground and I was fascinated by all the body-less legs passing the by the basement windows at incredible speed. Tired and still recuperating, I could not join my shipmates on a little sightseeing trip. At an afternoon tea and cake party, we were told that our departure for Chicago was to be that evening and we would be in an overnight sleeping car. That really created excitement in all of us. We were all going to the mid-West. Two to Chicago, I was one of them, and five to St. Louis and beyond. I was to meet my aunt and uncle, who had been in the US since 1927 when they emigrated with their three children, and my half sister Elizabeth (Elsie). They would take me to my new foster family, the day following our arrival.

November 25, 1934

Dearest Little Daughter,

Your letter on your arrival in Chicago we shared with the few friends who have the courage to come and see us. It is sad that so many whom we thought our friends painfully avoid us, but at least in the store we are still busy, more so because people are curious about you. Now you are with your sponsors, Dr. and Mrs. Sonnenschein, who sound like wonderful people. I'm sorry they don't speak German, but this way you will learn English much faster. Their welcome gift, the Shirley Temple Doll, sounds very beautiful. Don't think you're too old or sophisticated to play with it. Remember only a year ago, you and Ruth had tea parties with all your dolls, even made clothes for them to match your outfits. You say you live in a *Wolkenkratzer (Skyscraper)* and take an elevator to your apartment. It all sounds very elegant and luxurious, with their Spanish antiques and family mementoes. Be careful that you don't break anything, rushing around as you do. You must not feel humiliated being in a grade with younger children. It is, I am sure, only until you learn enough English to get along in your proper grade. Look what you have already learned: That Bret Harte (the name of your school) was an American author who wrote about western heroes, much like our own Karl May, and that the American number one sport is base-ball, according to the Comiskey children, who are teaching you all about it. You always enjoyed the Sportfests we had here in Germany, so you should the sports in your new country as well.

Please greet the Sonnenscheins and their friend Mr. Wolfe for us. Also write Elsie (she is rather lazy when it comes to writing) and Aunt Lydia. I know the latter will come to see you as soon as she is able to leave her job on a Sunday afternoon. She is so pleased with the new family that adopted you.

Write soon.

Your affectionate family and Papa

That time in my memory ...

As I mentioned before, I was welcomed to my new foster home on Chicago's South Side. I had my Aunt Lydia, mother's sister, and her family living in Chicago, as well as Aunt Lydia's mother-in-law and sister-in-law, whom I did not remember from Europe. They immigrated before 1927.

The trip to Chicago stands out very sharp in my memory. I remember waking to the clickety-clack of the overnight train to Chicago. Raising the window shade in my lower berth, I gasped to see a landscape gray and flat as I had never seen it before Here and there stood a clapboard house, a tree or a few bushes, not a gentle slope or hill in sight. As it was morning, we must have been outside of Chicago, somewhere in Indiana I suspected. I heard movement all around the coach, somewhere a muted gong sounded … breakfast. I dressed as quickly as I could, when our escort poked her head through the parted curtains and bid me a smiling good morning. The next two hours of breakfast, checking our belongings, briefings on our arrival flew by like pictures in a kaleidoscope. With each passing mile, the anticipation of what lay ahead grew. Finally, there was the bustle of a huge railway station-I tried to look everywhere to find some sense of peace and order but it all escaped me. Would it always be like that? All the voices around chattering in a language I couldn't understand. The train came to a stop with all of us ready to get off. I remember holding on to our escort as we stepped off to meet more committee members. Then I saw who I thought were my Aunt Lydia, Mamma's sister, and her husband. Of course, I had not seen them since 1927 when they emigrated to the U.S.; but their pictures and likenesses had kept us in familiar touch. Uncle Ernest had a bouquet of flowers, a very European gesture, although they looked so American in fashionable clothes. We laughed, we cried, we clasped each other with joy, all the while working our way through the big station hall and out to a car which my uncle pulled up with great pride. My cousins would be waiting for us at the hotel where they all lived and where my aunt and uncle were employed. On meeting them, I found they too had grown—quite Americanized, I thought. Herta, the eldest, was what I would term a "Backfisch" (a German word for fashionable teenager), the boys, Herbert, plump and mischievous, and Erwin, solemn and slight, all proclaiming: "we're real American kids now." Particularly this was emphasized when I tried to remind them how we stood mesmerized at their living room window one night, watching the Schupo (police) beat the communists in the street. Yes, they were "real American kids now" with their past all but forgotten. We had a lovely welcoming party in their rather small hotel apartment with all of uncle's relatives squeezed in. The next day, they were to deliver me to my new foster parents, Dr. and Mrs. Joseph B. Sonnenschein who lived on Chicago's South side in Jackson Towers, an elegant apartment skyscraper.

The following day, we went to my future home where we were met by a jolly elderly gentlemen and his handsome wife. They were the Sonnenscheins, Uncle Joe and Aunt Grace as I was to call them. Uncle Joe was a rotund little gentleman much in the image of the actor Edmund Gwen—gentle and smiling. Aunt Grace was what I would call patrician—all in silver and blue with carefully coiffed hair and elegant clothes. Her smile lit up her entire face, and I felt warm and comforted. They welcomed me with a beautiful Shirley Temple doll, Shirley being the most popular of

Hollywood stars of the moment. Other gifts included a popular girls' book, Anne of Green Gables, and a beautiful hat, scarf, and mitten set. Mamma had sent them some Belgian chocolates in a crystal box that had belonged to my grandmother, and that seemed very appropriate. The Sonnenscheins lived in a beautiful apartment filled with Spanish antiques, which also overawed me. This was located in a tower building across from what is now the Museum of Science and Industry in Jackson Park. At that time, the museum was know as the Rosenwald Museum and was a remnant of the 1893 Columbia Exposition. Although I was to share a huge bedroom with Aunt Grace, there was a corner of bookshelves, a desk, and chair all set aside for me. I had my own closet. The household also included a close friend, a retired lawyer named Harry Wolf, and an attractive black maid named Ophelia complete in black uniform, white cap, and dainty apron. She served us tea and cookies as we made attempts to get acquainted. Uncle Joe and Mr. Wolf knew a few German words, as both were in World War I, and with my Aunt and Uncle as interpreters, we got along quite well. Since the Sonnenscheins had no children, they really looked forward to my growing up in their home. I was to be enrolled in a small school just down the street, a school where most of the young professors of Chicago University were educating their children. It was called Bret Harte and only went through 5th grade. Since I knew no English (except a few polite phrases), I was to be placed in the 4th grade. I made up my mind then and there: not for long. I was determined to be in my own grade, the 7th.

Jackson Towers, an impressive apartment complex where I would be living, did not house many children. Most of the residents were well-to-do middle-aged couples, who could afford the prices. The children whom I remember best and with whom I played were the Comiskey children, who taught me all about baseball. Their father owned the Chicago White Sox baseball team. Our favorite pastime, besides visiting the Museum's coal mine, was riding up and down the elevators guessing what floor we were on, and skipping on the rocks at the lake shore.

I already introduced my Aunt Lydia and her family. She became my main source of communication with my family back home. It was through her, more than anyone else, including my own letters, that Mamma and Pappa knew what was happening to me. What was surprising was that I found my Uncle had so many relatives, all living in the Chicago area, relatives I never knew existed.

2

December 1934

HEADLINES OF THE DAY:

TOKYO—Japan Denounces Washington Naval Treaty of 1922; Calls Limitations on Japanese Naval Builds Unfair

ROME—Mussolini Rejects Mediation by League of Nations in Clash with Ethiopia

---

December 1934

Dearest Little Daughter,

What a beautiful time you must have had at your first Thanksgiving, quite a bit different from the Jewish Succoth and the German *Erntedankfest (German Thanksgiving)*. River Forest sounds very beautiful, particularly the way you described it with beautiful autumn colored leaves and blue skies, not at all like the bleak and cold November in Europe with rainy gray days. Mama was fascinated by the food that was served: Turkey, which is not as fat as goose but much bigger and meatier. Corn: yes, you are right; we don't eat that in Europe. It is only for the livestock, because it is so coarse and inedible here. Black olives: I suppose they came from Italy or Greece. Ah, Celery: again, I only know that we do not eat stalks here, they are bitter and flat. But you do remember Mama's celery root salad, which you so enjoyed. Cranberries sound much like the lingonberries we eat with Swedish pancakes. Pumpkin pie is something we should make from our fruit. The only recipe we have for pumpkin is for stews, which usually are not very palatable or appetizing. You see how much you have learned about the Pilgrims and their Thanksgiving celebration. We are all well and waiting for your letter. As we light our Chanukah candles, we think of you and take joy in your well-being.

With much love, your Pappa

That time in my memory …

Thanksgiving was in a beautiful home in River Forest, with relatives of Dr. and Mrs. Sonnenschein. About thirty people had gathered to welcome me. The food: The afore-mentioned turkey, sweet potato with marshmallow, cranberry sauce, celery, mince-meat and pumpkin pie, were all new and strange to me. The only familiar thing was the chicken soup. The old grandmother was very disappointed that I could understand only a few words of her Yiddish, which she thought was like German. It had a few words which I thought sounded like Plattdeutsch (colloquial German) I tried to follow her conversation, but it was hard to concentrate with all that was going on around me. The children attending were older, in their teens, and not at all interested in the little girl from overseas. There must have been thirty people, at least. All of them were relatives of the Sonnenscheins.

Some I got to know quite well over the years, particularly, Uncle Joe's two sisters and one nephew, who also lived in Chicago. One sister, Madame Roe, as she was known, was a voice teacher in Chicago. It was she and Uncle Joe who discovered that

I could sing and started me on vocal lessons. Uncle Joe, himself, had a beautiful tenor voice and sang in one of the synagogues on Chicago's South Side. One of their close friends was a glorious contralto named Marie Barova, whose career spanned Europe and the United States. I so wanted to be like her, and was thrilled by all her encouragement.

For Chanukah, I lit my own candles on a brand new Menorah, with Uncle Joe and Mr. Wolf joining me in the age-old ritual and songs. Aunt Grace, who was Christian, stood by with lots of presents, which somehow she had accumulated for everyone. She in turn was overwhelmed by the gift Uncle Joe and I had selected for her at Marshall Fields, that magical store in downtown Chicago. To be perfectly frank, I don't think they had ever had a Chanukah celebration in their house before, but it was festive and warm, and made me forget my homesickness for a little while.

December 15, 1934

Dearest Little Thea:

Thank you for your birthday greeting to me and also for the one to Ruth. Those were beautiful cards you made. As for the picture, the turkey looks very appetizing and everybody around the table looks so happy, you seemed to fit right in. We hope the package you sent does not get lost as so many packages from overseas do. It is impossible to send foodstuff as it disappears in the first post-office it passes through.

We now are obligated to have a patriotic, once-a-week *Eintopf Gericht*[1]. If you don't want to cook it yourself, you can bring your pot to a feeding station, where along with the meal, you get a propaganda film about the heroes of the Third Reich. We had a special celebration with Mamma's apple cake and whip cream, which she managed to assemble in exchange for something from our garden.

Every week there is a new order to make it harder for Jews to make a living. Except for a few shirkers, people want to pay their debts to me even some who have not paid for years. We all have colds, but my one Schnapps at night is good medicine and there is always Mamma's excellent chamomile tea.

How is your English coming along? By now, you should be able to talk to your classmates much better. It is so much easier for young people to learn a new language, than for us older ones. They are not handicapped by the correctness of grammar and the content or subject matter; never mind the mistakes. They will correct themselves with time.

Write soon again we love you very much—

Your devoted Pappa

That time in my memory …

Although every week brought new restrictions, Pappa was still on the city council and the local Nazis were not too anxious to enforce them and force him off. He had joined the City Council when Uncle Ernest left for the U.S. in 1927. His loyal friends always voted him in, even though Hitler was now head of the government and discouraged any Jewish participation therein. The Eintopf Gericht, one pot meal, was an

---

1.   The new and patriotic one pot meal; a stew of vegetable and meat, if it was available, it was encouraged by the Nazis to be eaten as a tribute to the New Order.

excellent public relations ploy that Goebbels devised to get families into the Nazi ranks.

Meanwhile, I settled in at the Sonnenscheins. Schoolwork was a struggle. "What means" became my favorite, often used, phrase, but the teachers continued to encourage my questioning. Although, I was building a basic vocabulary, my grammar was atrocious. Still, unlike adults who are learning, I wasn't afraid to use it with all its faults. My accent was also the cause of much tittering and joking around the classroom and I hated it. I was crushed by being called "a kraut" and complained to my foster parents. They sympathized but felt they could do nothing about it. I didn't realize that in spite of Fritz Kuhn and his Nazi followers, there was still a lot of anti-German sentiment. It seemed strange that in Germany we were considered non-German even though our families had been there since the 16th Century, and in the U.S. we were considered German aliens. It was most bewildering to me.

We had a wonderful holiday celebration at the Del Prado Hotel in Hyde Park. I observed that, even with their beautiful homes, so many people celebrated holidays in hotels. Later I learned that hotel entertaining was a status symbol for the upper middle class.

That puzzled me: I thought, no matter how beautiful and elegant the hotel, it can never replace celebrations in one's own home.

December, 30 1934

Dearest Little Daughter,

This is the last of 1934; but what will 1935 bring? I dare not think of it, but take joy in knowing that you are so safe. It sounds like you had a wonderful Chanu-kah/Christmas celebration with a theater party and many gifts. Your American chocolate bars arrived and Ruth will not eat them, especially the ones called "Baby Ruth." She shows them around proudly, a candy in the United States named after her. She and Mamma made gingerbread with lots of spices, raisins and fruit, since sugar is hard to get. Don't forget the potato pancakes and applesauce, which are always family favorites. Mamma's scarf, as well as mine, is beautiful and warm. We certainly can use them in this cold weather. Gerda will come to visit before she goes to the U.S. or to Brazil to continue her medi-cal studies. They are trying to work out an arrangement, whereby she will be allowed to go as long as Wolfgang remains in Germany. It is a very tragic situa-tion.

"What will the New Year bring?" Everybody asks the same question. At least, more Jews are asking this themselves, and we have more parents worried about the safety of their children. Optimistically, but foolishly perhaps, some still feel nothing bad will happen to them, even with Hitler in charge of the Gov-ernment. I think otherwise

I know you are sometimes lonely and long to be with other children; that is only natural; but think of the great museum across the park from where you live and the fun you seem to have there. It's a wonderful learning experience. You say that there is a real coalmine and you spend a lot of time in it. Tell us more about it: Coalmining in Europe is a very dangerous occupation, but I'm sure that your model mine is safe for visitors.

Eating roasted chestnuts, while ice-skating on the midway, sound like a won-derful adventure, too. Surely you do this with many friends. I know when you catch up with your proper grade you will have a lot of classmates your own age. The new semester is not far away and you have something to anticipate.

We will drink a hearty Glühwein[2] to the New Year quietly and wish for the well being of all our dear ones.

With love, your devoted Pappa, Mamma and Ruth

---

2.   The traditional mulled wine was everyone's favorite drink for seeing in the New Year. That reminded me of Germany.

That time in my memory ...

My other half-sister, Gerda, who was studying medicine in Leipzig, was dismissed from the institute of medical studies. What was even more devastating: her marriage to a prominent German doctor was terminated. Looking back on this tragedy, her husband was literally held as a hostage in his job at the hospital while she would be allowed to go to the U.S. or Brazil to continue her studies. Here we'd call it black-mail. As it turned out, after the divorce, she went to Brazil, where it was easier for the German government to provide a sponsor for her. Ironically, the Nazi regime paid for her continued medical training.

One of the memorable highlights of the winter of '34–'35 was the ice-skating on the midway by the University of Chicago. The sunken lawns were flooded and frozen into skating surfaces with lights rigged around them. Besides the Comiskey children, I had become friends with some of the university professor's children, who were my age or older. The parents were particularly interested in the experiment in education in which I took part. The good weather found us skating with lights and music, eating roasted chestnuts and burnt almonds, and drinking hot chocolate at the edge of the ice. One thing I found a nuisance: you had to attach your skates to sturdy shoes—there were no skating shoes as there are today.

Another outstanding event that became a yearly tradition was a Christmas luncheon, hosted by Aunt Grace, at Marshall Fields Department Store, with a performance of "A Christmas Carol" afterwards. This became a yearly tradition, lasting long into my adulthood.

Pappa's remarks about the German New Year began to create a sense of impending dread in me: Somehow I rationalized that although I was safe—the safer I became, the more danger I foresaw for my family and friends. These fears were to overshadow all my thoughts for the next three years.

Apparently, as Pappa indicated, I was not alone in my foreboding: German Jews were beginning to see the true course of Nazi anti-Semitism. Minor restrictions had been imposed against German Jews from the beginning of the Nazi regime, but they caused little consternation. Hitler defended them as "temporary" measures and kept up a campaign of rhetoric against foreign Jewry to camouflage his real intentions against German Jews.

Yet, as each month and year passed, the minor restrictions became major ones: Jews were forbidden access to public transit and facilities. They were taken out of important and visible occupations and relegated to minor ones. All of the great Jewish physicians, jurists, musicians, and artists were the targets of Nazi campaigns; Jewish politicians had already been largely silenced or eliminated.

3

January 1935

HEADLINES OF THE DAY:

GENEVA—Ethiopia Asks League of Nations to Guard Peace with Italy

MOSCOW—U.S.S.R. Doubles Its Army to 940,000

GERMANY—Saar Plebiscite Shows 90.8% Favor return to Germany

GENEVA—League of Nations Votes to Award Germany the Saar Basin on March 1

BERLIN—Germany Announces Reich Steel Production up 104% in Year since Hitler's Ascendance

WASHINGTON—FDR, in State of the Union Address, Says Government Will Provide Jobs for 3.5 Million on Welfare

January 1935

My Dear Child,

Now we can write the year 1935, and you are in your new home for almost two months. The note from Dr. and Mrs. Sonnenschein put us much at ease. They sound so happy to have you bring youth and joy into their home. Their families also sound delighted that you are with them, since they never had children of their own.

Since you left, there have been quite a few changes. People come to the store because they are curious about what has happened to you. Apparently, the government knows very little concerning the children's transports. At least, it has not tried to stop them. People now think I may not have been so crazy, after all, putting an ocean between us.

We've visited the Stiefel family in Grünstadt. Their son Manfred is eager to leave. I hope he is successful in Stuttgart, as Visas are more and more difficult to get. I told him to contact Family Neuberger who was so kind to you when you had to go to the consulate. Although the people at the consulate were impersonal and unsympathetic, you had that wonderful family encouraging you with their hospitality. Always remember, people are basically kind and trustworthy. The proof is where you are now and what is being done for you.

Your schoolmates, especially Elfriede, send greetings. I am sorry they were all punished for coming to the railroad station to see you off. I hope you pressed at least one of those roses they brought you, but I suppose some of them wearing their Nazi youth uniforms for their farewell to you was not such a good idea. I wonder who reported them.

Since Mamma wants to write a few lines and so does Gerda and Ruth, I must close. I also have a meeting with Mr. Heilmann, who wants to help us where he can. His sons are fine boys who are not afraid to speak out.

Please greet the Sonnenscheins for us and do well at school. I know it is difficult when you don't know the language, but soon you will be in your real grade. Again, write a letter to your little sister. She is very lonesome for you and so eager to know about your new life. It is only too bad she was not old enough to go with you. Did you know the wonderful museum you go to in the afternoon was part of the Columbia Exposition in 1893? Not many children know that and you are able to go there and enjoy it and all its treasures.

Until next time—

Your Pappa, with love.

That time in my memory ...

Some of my former classmates, who came to see me off, were questioned by the Chief of Police as to why they "farewelled" a little Jewish girl with a bouquet of roses and tears. Elfriede and Senna were singled out for questioning. He also questioned them as to what was said, and did they all go to our house afterward? None of the teachers or clergy was called in, only the children. Mr. Heilmann, the liberal editor of the local newspaper, and his sons were constantly reminded to toe the party line in their publication. He was a very good friend of my father's.

Here, I continued to make progress in English, encouraged in particular by the many professors Uncle Joe knew at University of Chicago. Aunt Grace took me to see many classic movies to help me with my English. She was a nurse in World War I when she met and married Uncle Joe, a physician in that war. Most of her family lived in the Pittsburgh area where we were to visit for Easter.

The museum across the park was then called the Rosenwald Museum. It had been built for the Columbia Exposition of 1893 and was one of the showpieces of Chicago. In later years, it became the Museum of Science and Industry. It never ceased to fascinate me and even though I visited it alone many times, I was never bored. I particularly liked the coal mine, which was a wonderful place to play "hide and seek." Many years later, when I took my own children there, it was a real German WWII submarine that was the highlight of the exhibits.

January 29, 1935

Dear Thea,

Your letter came in record time on Thursday. Usually it arrives Saturday or Monday. So I want to answer it right away. Healthwise, we are in good shape though winter is taking its toll. Since we don't socialize very much we are spared the usual colds and coughs. I am still taking the train to Frankenthal because of my eyes and hopefully will receive my glasses shortly. I am thankful I have a Jewish optometrist in Dr. Rahlston, as the others are not allowed to treat Jews. Interesting enough the Jewish Doctors can still treat Germans with certain stipulations, but most of them are reluctant to do so as they can be accused of "professional misdemeanor" by anybody at anytime.

We are curious what is happening at school. Have you joined your real grade? You must not worry about your accent and that some of the children call you "Kraut." It is better than being called a "dirty Jew."

Gerda is still with us before she leaves for South America. She still has hopes of coming to the U.S.A. She had such plans for you to come to Leipzig some day and study medicine as she did. But you will make your own way, no matter what you study. Please write Ruth a separate letter. She sees so few children outside of our neighbors these days. Thank G-d, Herr Lehrer Steuer, who is now the principal, insists on her staying in school, despite some of the Nazi teachers' objections and grumblings.

About Elsie, she wrote after a long silence. She is moving from Los Angeles to Chicago to get a job near you. However, she is very vague about it. Aunt Lydia and the Lowensteins wrote that they visited you and that you are so well taken care of that we should not worry. You do not need to feel guilty that they must work so hard and you don't. Uncle Ernest has a good job as a building engineer and Aunt Lydia runs the housekeeping office in the same hotel, so they are very content. Your cousins do not expect you to give them anything of your allowance or your gifts. The boys, in particular, so don't worry so about having so much more.

We send you our love as always—your Pappa

That time in my memory ...

Father had developed cataracts. Fortunately, there was a prominent Jewish ophthalmologist in Frankenthal; otherwise he would not have been treated. By that time no Aryan doctor was allowed to have Jewish patients. As for Gerda, although she still had hopes of coming to the United States, she was still in limbo, waiting to hear if she would go there or to Brazil. Her divorce devastated her, but she had resigned herself to the facts of life: better Brazil than a concentration camp.

My complaint about being called a "Kraut", I realize now, was because of my atrocious German accent and was not malicious. Dad's comment made my acceptance of the situation somewhat easier, and I tried to joke about it myself. I had not yet joined my regular grade. It was decided to keep me in the 4ᵗʰ grade, rather than send me down the road to Hyde Park and enter me into my proper one. My English was still too sketchy, they felt, although my math had advanced to its proper level. I still had very few friends my own age. Actually, I was more thrilled with the attention of the adults surrounding Uncle Joe in philosophical discussions at least twice a week. Aunt Grace couldn't understand why I preferred them to my Shirley Temple doll.

I was not at ease with my aunt and uncle's family. I felt strained with my cousins and their curiosity into my life with the Sonnenscheins. I seemed to have so much more than they had, and I felt that every time they admired something I had, I should give it to them. At Holiday time, I received a silver pin, and gave it to my cousin Herta when she admired it so. My aunt Lydia made her return it. I felt so ashamed that after that I wore no more jewelry except Mamma's Shaddai and a little pinky ring when I visited them.

Elsie was still an unknown quantity. She was always called the "wild one", and I wondered how her settling in Chicago would impact on my life. She had come to the U.S. with my aunt and uncle and was in the tradition of Isadora Duncan, "a free spirit." California suited her, and I couldn't understand why she wanted to come to Chicago to be near me and feel restricted. She always was the instigator in my troubles with Mamma, but this was many years later and I hoped she had settled down. She had studied nursing and had been nurse/companion to several well-to-do ladies on the West Coast.

4

February 1935

HEADLINES OF THE DAY:

FLEMINGTON, N.J.—Bruno Richard Hauptmann Found Guilty in Lindbergh Kidnapping

ROME—While League of Nations Debates in Geneva, Mussolini Mobilizes 35,000 Troops for Duty in Africa

BERLIN—Hitler Opens World's Largest Auto Show in Berlin

VIENNA—Violinist Fritz Kreisler Confesses to Musical Hoax

February 4, 1935

Dear little Thea,

Your letter arrived as usual with much awaited hope and anxiety. Ruth delivered all your greetings and messages to the proper recipients, who were delighted to receive them. I report our state of health is good, and I can only hope the same from you, that you have plenty of opportunity to enjoy the great outdoors. I can only imagine what "frozen rock-hopping" must be like on the Chicago lakefront. We were in Frankenthal again where Dr. Rahlston pronounced my eyes in good condition. We have developed a beautiful friendship in these trying times when one's former friends disillusion and desert you. But we are still lucky—Mr. Heilmann and Dr. Ludwig, the Mayor, could not be more loyal, as are many of my clients. We now get many calls from parents who would like their children out of harm's way—the last being the Stiefels and Kleinbergers (Elfriede). We are getting visits from many relatives, as that is the best way to keep up each other's courage.

We're deep into winter, and it sets the mood for the many anti-Jewish regulations that come out day by day. There are still people who think they will be exempted from some of the harsher laws because they know someone important. I think that is a false assumption. When it comes to the final reckoning, it will all be the same, whether you contributed to society, whether you're one-quarter Jewish, or whom you know in government. Quatsch!!(Nonsense, which was one of Pappa's favorite words)

Hope your winter is going well with school uppermost in the picture. I can only imagine your day-to-day joy without fear.

Always with love—your Pappa

Remembrances and Reflections:

After the Reichstag fire (February 27, 1933), more and more daily and weekly laws were issued—so many that a bewildered public could not cope with them unless the uniformed S.A. or S.S. drove the lesson home with public demonstrations.

The demonstrations could be anything from a torchlight parade to the boycott and harassment of Jewish businesses. A very popular one was the public humiliation of couples who were committing "Rassenschande", very often involving a Jewish man whose lover was a non-Jewish woman. The pressure on many mixed marriage couples was indescribable. My own sister, Gerda, was one of those whose husband was blackmailed into divorcing her. Even a prostitute could be made virtuous by claiming to have been approached by a Jew and then turning him over to the authorities. Debts to Jewish merchants could be automatically cancelled. Pappa became more and more involved with helping families contact the HIAS for their children's exit papers (A thorough description of HIAS and its mission can be found in "Never Wave Goodbye" by Iris Posner and Philip Jason).

My own life here ran on a pretty predictable routine of school, studying, and a fairly quiet social life evolving around Uncle Joe and Aunt Grace's friends. The rock hopping Pappa refers to was really a forbidden pastime, since it might become danger-ous. The huge rocks that bounded Lake Michigan became slippery with the frozen spray off the lake. It was great fun to slide from one to the other on a piece of corru-gated cardboard, until one of the children got hurt and we were no longer allowed to do so. We still had skating on the midway, Saturday movies and shopping trips, which had become the norm for me. I became very conscious of the gulf between what my life was, and that of my little sister, who lived with a lot of fears. I tried to block them out with books and my beloved daily soap operas. Ironically, they too contributed to my knowledge of English, in spite of their fantastic plots and dramatics.

Meanwhile, I loved my voice lessons. I thought I knew a lot of German songs, but Madame Roe knew a lot more. She was an expert on Lotte Lehmann, having studied with her and Marie Barova in Germany. Madame Ernestine Schumann-Heink and Kirsten Flagstad were my ideals of perfect singers, but I knew very little about Ameri-can opera singers until later in my studies.

Eisenberg, February 18, 1935

Dear Little Thea-

Though I didn't write in Mamma's letter last week you know my thoughts were with you. Mr. Heilmann thought it would be a good idea to visit all our relatives, and so Cousin Max picked me up Monday morning and we took the "Grand Tour", beginning with the relatives in Trier. We went on to Wawern and on to Heusweiler. On Sunday we visited the relatives in Homburg/Saar. All are concerned what the Saar annexation will mean to them. You can imagine how eager they were to hear news of you and they all want to be remembered. I arrived home last night and even as tired as I was, I was overjoyed to find two letters from you. There are so many questions from everyone. I don't know where to begin. You must send us a day-by-day account of your activities: No matter how trivial they may seem to you, they are important to us.

There have been new administrative directives pertaining to non-Jews who work for Jews and members in the National Socialist Party who buy from Jews. For example, a Jew may no longer address a Christian, even a friend of long standing, by his first name. Furthermore, it is considered immoral to buy anything from Jews, unless they are the only handlers of that product.

More children are leaving, which is good. They all want to contact you, but as they may not be going to Chicago, their contact to you may be doubtful. While I was gone, there was the usual "harassment" at the store. Having an "Aryan" manager certainly has its advantages.

Yes, the children are leaving, but at the same time, life goes on, and more are being born. The Michel family has great joy in a son, born ten days ago and so we shall all celebrate this event. We have so few joyous events; we make the most of those we do have. For today we all send our love. Ruth asks you not to forget to write the relatives and send pictures.

With devoted kisses—Your Pappa

That time in my memory ...

Whenever Pappa was made aware by his friends that official or Nazi party harassment was in the offing, he conveniently left to visit our numerous relatives. The Aryan manager to whom he refers was, I believe, a Mrs. Kemp, an indomitable lady who, being over forty years of age, could still work for a Jewish concern. Besides Pappa, there were only three other Jewish merchants in town: the Schwarzschilds, who owned a butcher shop; the Froehlichs—who had a home furnishing and clothing emporium;

and our Aunt Rosa—who was the proprietor of a man's haberdashery and a woman's hat shop. Aunt Rosa, (Tante Rosa as we all called her) was really no blood relative of ours, though she lived with us. She had been engaged to one of Mamma's brothers who died in the war and so we became her family. I can picture her, always fashionably dressed, more like a French woman than a German, and surrounded by the scents of violets and lavender. Thus, there was not that much competitive harassment by the Christian merchants, who had successful businesses of their own.

I passed another milestone in my school career. I was placed in 5th grade, which was better than being in 4th. Actually, I did not mind too much, as I would've had to leave Bret Harte School for my proper grade at Hyde Park School. By now I had become quite used to the school being in walking distance, the friendly, helpful teachers, and yes, even the classmates, who stopped teasing me. Aunt Grace had given a class Valentine party and that helped enormously in breaking down barriers between me and the other children.

February 26, 1935

My Dear Little Daughter,

Though we received no letter this week, we assume that everything is all right with you. The heavy storms raging on the ocean, no doubt, contribute to the delay in the mail. Although there have been outbreaks of Grippe and other winter illnesses, we seem to be bypassed since we have so few social contacts. So something good can be said of our isolation. Tante Lydia and Grandmother Lowenstein said that Elsie is trying to get a job in Chicago to be near you. Ruth asks daily about the package you offered to send. She looks forward to it with great anticipation.

The end of the week I am traveling to Heusweiler again to help your Uncle Herman in his business. As you must have heard Saar is now part of Germany again, and they expect the same problems that trouble the Jews in Germany. We congratulate you that you were put in 5th grade, which means you must be making great progress in your English. Your playmates in your building sound very nice. Imagine, riding an elevator up and down instead of a bicycle. You speak of the father owning a baseball team in Chicago. Is that a business like owning a store? I cannot imagine making money doing that.

Ruth has several school days off in celebrating the Saar annexation. Naturally all the children (except she) are expected to participate in all day celebrations for this event. She is very lonely, please write her more. She gets thinner all the time and does not sleep well. She wanted to knit you a BDM jacket[1]but we thought it would not be a good idea and persuaded her to make something with daisies on it. Please, please, write all your news. Although you are disappointed at not having your own room, it sounds lovely where you are, especially the corner for all your books and toys. Gerda is still with us and as you can imagine is sad indeed. We hope the change to South America will be good for her.

With devoted love and kisses—your Pappa

That time in my memory:

The Comiskeys, who lived in the same building, were the owners of the Chicago White Sox team, and Pappa was concerned if indeed a living could be made by playing base-

---

1.   The *Bund Deutscher Mädchen's* (League of German Girls) official uniform was a sweater for German girls in black, red, and green colors. It was a colorful topping of girls' drab, mustard-colored uniform that now was required.

ball: *Racing cars, Boxing, Skiing, and Soccer were indeed money making sports. But baseball? As we all know here in the United States, it is a very good business. Tom and his sister, Dorothy, became my sources of information on everything American.*

By now, I had acclimated myself to the Sonnenschein household, but I was still very much alone since I couldn't always participate in the adult social life that involved them. A great solace was Ophelia, who spent the evenings with me. She made me very much aware of the contrast between Black and White America. It puzzled me that unlike the vicious discrimination that existed in Germany, there were subtle laws, nuances that ruled the lives of the "colored."

There were of course, also very brutal acts, such as the lynchings in the South. Whereas the Jews had been accepted in European society, the black man had never been accepted here. I know I always felt bad when Ophelia told me about the sad lot of her many relatives who had come from the South and settled in Chicago, as a city of opportunity. Anywhere else, Ophelia could have been an elegant lady, but not here. I remember visiting her mother one Sunday afternoon, and having tea with a charming lady, who could have been anyone's mother and/or sister. Their skin was beautifully deep gold and their features were anything but Negroid. It's hard to believe that many areas and places were closed to them, as they were for all the Jews in Germany. Her mother's mantle piece was full of family photographs, and I remember one very dignified gentleman who was said to be working in the White House. I'm glad Aunt Grace gave me a box of chocolates to present to Ophelia's mother. She in turn gave me a lovely handkerchief as a remembrance. I've never forgotten the grace of that visit to Ophelia's mother on a snowy February afternoon.

5

March 1935

HEADLINES OF THE DAY:

SAAR BASIN—Germany Celebrates Return of the Saar Territory to Germany

UNITED STATES—2,000 Arrested in Surprise Raid on Organized Crime

GERMANY—Hitler Renounces Treaty of Versailles Restrictions, Reinstates Military Conscription

BERLIN—Germany Orders Arrest of 700 Pastors for Expounding Jesus' Jewish Birth

INDIA—British Fire on 20,000 Rioting Moslems, Killing 23

BERLIN—Hitler Says Soviets Imperil Peace in Europe

LONDON—Britain & Russia Agree on Treaties to Curb German Reich

March 3, 1935

Dear little Thea,

Today, your letter from the 20th arrived, and we can always tell when we have mail from you. The postman makes us the first customers on his route, even before he brings money to anybody.

At this time, I am also writing Aunt Lydia, Grandmother, and Elsie. I have held up all my correspondence until your package arrived. It finally came on Wednesday. What a joy! Naturally, the one who had the greatest pleasure was Ruth, since she was the main recipient of all the things you sent. As always, it's good to hear from you. I know it is not always easy and convenient for such a busy young lady to write. But you are a dutiful daughter who knows how much we wait for your letters.

With the celebration for the annexation of the Saar, all stores are closed, and there are torchlight parades every night. We are fortunate to be Jewish, as we don't have to march or answer to the party why we didn't march. We have a lot of rain and a flu epidemic. Again we are saved, with so little social contact we are spared illnesses that affect everyone else, but then we don't have to be in on every misery.

Fastnacht[1] is upon us. At least it gives us some relief from the politics and the endless harassment. Mamma made her famous stuffed pancakes, but there are no sharp, critically funny speeches as there have been in the past. Even the famous ones like Köln, Mainz, and Frankfurt seem to have lost their bite. Everyone is so afraid to offer an opinion critical of the government even in a lighthearted way.

Gerda would love to have a letter in English so she can practice it with you. She is still waiting to hear from South America about her immigration. Mamma says to tell you that Ruth is much happier to go to bed now that she has the beautiful Betty Boop pajamas you sent. And she loves to hear about the entertaining American cartoons, as you call them. All of those are not available to the children here. What a pity; they have so little enjoyment as it is.

Write soon again. Much Love—

Pappa and your family

---

1.   Shrove Tuesday/Mardi Gras

That time in my memory …

The Mardi Gras is a time for merriment as well as the biting satirical "Buttenreden", a political roast in most of the large cities all over Germany. It was now strictly forbidden to make jokes about the government, thus dampening the spirit of the festivities. The annexation of the Saar Basin was a great triumph for the Germans—much more celebrated in Germany itself than in the annexed territory. Mardi Gras, the beginning of Lent, was not the joyous holiday it had always been, but took on political overtones with fiery patriotic speeches instead of the critical satires, the "Buttenreden", which had been a German tradition for centuries.

I was so glad that Aunt Grace thought of the Betty Boop pajamas for Ruth. The popular cartoon character was the answer to Ruth's nightly "I-don't-want-to-go-to-bed" routine and provided her a special incentive to follow our parents' wishes.

At this time, we were introduced to a show-and-tell period at school. We were asked to talk about our favorite book or history character. It gave everyone a chance to be "on stage" for the moment, and I loved it. Naturally, it became my favorite class time and reluctance to go to school became a thing of the past. Instead of the classic Becky Thatcher that all of the girls tried to emulate, I opted for the heroic son of William Tell, the one who had the apple shot from his head. This was keeping in character with all of the heroes I admired. Naturally, very few pupils in my class had heard of the son of William Tell. At that time in my adolescence, I admired all men of spirit who spoke the truth. Martyrdom was the highest aspiration. Strangely enough, I was not quite as knowledgeable about the women who achieved this status—that came later as I became more aware of their role in American history.

March 12, 1935

Dear little Thea,

It seems like nobody can answer your letters but me. Dear Mamma is too busy with the household, Gerda at the moment is at the interview in Hamburg, and little Ruth is afraid her handwriting is not good enough for you. *Alles Ausreden (All excuses, one of Pappa's favorite expressions for non-participation)*, oh well.

I just returned from Heusweiler, where again I helped Uncle Herman with the business. There was an open market-day and business was very brisk. Don't forget Uncle Herman has a lot of business with French goods, and the Germans prefer them over their own.

But that's enough about business which in my world becomes more restricted every day. Your greetings to teachers and schoolmates must wait until school opens again. It has been closed because of serious *Grippe* and influenza outbreaks. The weather isn't helping any; it's cold and miserable.

You still can go skating on your midway with your friends, I presume. You mention a friend of Dr. Joe's, who is the son-in-law of Thomas Mann. Do you know his name? You know Dr. Mann is one of our most famous German writers. So you see, not all people who leave Germany are Jews. Many of the artists and musicians leave of their own free will. You can be very proud to be in their company. Please send us a new picture. You have grown but you grumble that you're still one of the smallest and have to walk in front row in your gym class. Never mind. Stand tall and know you're doing us all proud.

Lovingly—Your, Pappa

That time in my memory …

So far, the annexation of the Saar had made no impact on Uncle Herman's business, but he, too, projected a changing future for him and his daughter's family. They were looking forward to leaving the Saarland and resettling in a country under a more moderate political regime.

Thomas Mann was one of the most famous German writers. His family chose to go into exile in Switzerland and the USA. I believe it was a Professor Borghese who was teaching at the University of Chicago and had married one of Thomas Mann's daughters. He was also a friend of Uncle Joe. The Sonnenscheins acquainted me through articles and books with many of the well-known people who had left Germany because of personal convictions and not necessarily religious persecution. The aforesaid Thomas Mann was one; Arturo Toscanini was another: The great Italian conductor refused to work in Nazi Germany. So were Max Reinhardt, Franz Werfel, and Oskar Kokoschka, who went into self-imposed exile. Others were so persecuted that they were driven to commit suicide, Ludwig Kirschner being one of them. I was indeed in very good company. This kept me from feeling like a "poor refugee", indeed.

March 18, 1935

Dear Little One,

As always, your letter arrived on time. You are so good about writing the letters which we await with great joy. Here, we are still in the grips of winter with influenza all around us. School is still closed, and Ruth is bored. I'm taking her with me on my customer trip tomorrow, which should be a nice change for her. Your Aunt Delphine is here, and this keeps Mamma busy and sociable.

I'm glad to hear you're making such good progress in English. Never mind the children laughing at your accent. There is a famous story about an Italian professor (it might even be Dr. Sonnenschein's friend, Prof. Borghese) who was interviewed by the newspapers about his accomplishments. One of the reporters remarked smugly: "Gee Professor, you speak pretty broken English." The Professor smiled and said in his strong accent, "Yes, and I speak 16 other languages, equally broken." It is what you have to say that is important, and that you can communicate it to others.

In the last months, no children left for the U.S. and parents are getting anxious. We were so lucky to have entered the program when we did, as it gets more difficult day by day.

Greetings from all the relatives. I know you cannot write to all of them on a steady basis but do remember them once in a while. Your classmates are still curious about what you're doing and the life you live in the United States, a veritable "Schlaraffenland" (land of magic and fantasy).

Your loving Pappa

That time in my memory ...

Dr. Sonnenschein had many friends among the faculty of the University of Chicago. Uncle Joe was Clinical Director for the Board of Health in that city, functioning under Dr. Herman Bundesen. I really enjoyed the adults in Uncle Joe's circle of friends. They were much more interested in my background than the children of my own age, which is understandable. As time went on, I met more children and joined them for "Lunch at Field's", concerts, and movies after my singing lessons. Madame Roe was a wonderful teacher who concentrated on the technique of German Lieder, which suited me fine as I was not that terribly interested in opera at the time. She gave me a book of Lotte Lehmann's, a leading German soprano, who became my ideal as a singer—a book of songs I still treasure.

School was getting easier and as much as I wanted to be with my own age group, I still remained in 5th grade.

Aunt Grace's relatives were here from Pittsburgh. They were wonderful and brought me many useful gifts, such as books on US History. I was not surprised to learn that Aunt Grace wasn't Jewish, as this happened so often in German-Jewish families. In the United States, it didn't seem to matter, but now it had tragic consequences in Germany. Hitler caused more tragedies, by splitting loving families than through any of his other edicts. We have a report on one of the families Pappa knew, who actually allowed the government to place their daughter in a concentration camp to separate her from her Jewish fiancé. He, of course, disappeared. What a horrible tragedy! I have already mentioned my own sister's marriage that was ended by government edict.

6

April 1935

HEADLINES OF THE DAY:

ADDIS ABABA—Ethiopian Troops Mass on Border with Italian Somalia

ITALY—Stresa Conference Opens to Discuss German Threat

GERMANY—Reich Chamber of Writers Excludes All Non-Aryan Members

BERLIN—Reich High Court Upholds Hitler's Plea for Non-Belief in Nazism as Grounds for Divorce

---

April 5, 1935

Dear Little Daughter,

We finally received your letters from 20 and 25 March and were delighted that you are so busy. Although you didn't understand it all, it must have been very interesting to be in an American Court of Justice. Dr. Sonnenschein was what is called a witness, who must swear under oath to tell only the truth. The fact that you did not understand the case is not important. What is important is you saw the American justice system at work. You are very lucky to meet his friend, the judge, and that they took you to lunch at their club. That is something very American and although I belonged to a *Brüderschaft*[1] with the city council, I am no longer a member there as I had to give up my position on the council. As Dr. Ludwig stated, "I was regrettably replaced."

You must not mind too much about the misunderstanding with Elsie and Aunt Lydia. They feel left out of your life, but you cannot live theirs and they cannot live yours. Gerda is in a job with a doctor in Bremen and is still uncertain about her future, whether it will be in Brazil or the United States. She is still suffering from the effects of her forced divorce from Wolfgang.

Mamma is already hard at spring cleaning. That never changes; the house must be immaculate from top to bottom. Since she no longer gets out as much socially, she is really throwing herself into the well-being of all of us.

Meanwhile, all our love to you.

Your devoted Pappa

That time in my memory …

It is amazing how my mother changed from a fairly easy-going social butterfly to a dedicated housewife. With the lack of help, the huge house still had to be kept in tip-top order. She still had the ever-loyal Lenchen, who, with her father, lived rent-free in the attic rooms and was still allowed to work for her.

The relationship with my half sister and my aunt became somewhat strained at that time. Whenever I did something they didn't approve of, they would complain to my parents. It meant that visiting them at times became awkward.

As for my life with the Sonnenscheins, it went blissfully in its way. Dr. Joe, in his capacity as a physician in the city's Medical Department, had to give testimony in

---

1.   Brotherhood, a men's group with similar ideas and interests.

many juried court cases. For one of them, I was allowed to accompany him. However, I had to stay in the judge's chambers, since it pertained to testimony regarding a rape case. Although I didn't understand what it was all about, I was not allowed in the court room. Meeting with his friend the judge afterwards for lunch, it was explained to me that the justice system protects all its victims, especially if they were minors. So this trial was closed to the public. It was a very impressive lesson about the workings of our justice system and made me feel very secure.

It was no surprise, and long expected that Pappa had to resign from the city council, where he had been active since 1927. His friends on that board remained very loyal. He took the decision with his usual good grace, not in bitterness, and he was still kept abreast of all the council's rulings the evening they were passed.

We were getting ready to go to Pittsburgh, and since we were to stay past vacation time, I was to take all my future homework with me. It made me feel very grown-up and aware of an increasing role in fulfilling my responsibilities.

April 15, 1935

Dear Little Daughter,

As always your letter is most heartily welcomed. To us it is more important than the latest political edicts that come out daily as to the dealing with Jews. Apparently it hasn't made as big an impression on the Saarländers, as many have French leanings.

We still are waiting for a picture from you. Don't you like to take snapshots any more? Do you remember how eagerly you collected 4 marks with the letters that spelled A.G.F.A. so you could get your first camera and how we had to stop you from snapping everybody in the bathtub?

You never wrote if you receive an allowance. We know that all your material things are taken care of. The reason I ask is that your cousin Gretel from Landstuhl, now in Indianapolis, wrote home for pocket money, but perhaps she spends more than she should.

Mamma is hard at her house cleaning. We are expecting a lot of company for the eight days of Pesach, and I will give services as usual with all the hospitality Mamma can muster. Thanks to the good neighbors who help her with that.

You write of wanting your books. Perhaps you will choose which ones, as Ruth has now taken possession of most of them. Last weekend was Protestant confirmation, an occasion when we usually sell most of the children's clothes. This year the pastor declared that it is "immoral" to buy these articles from Jews; and he could not with a clear conscience confirm a child whose parents did so. We sold only two (out of 10). They were to my manager, Mrs. Kempf, for her nephew and niece. We were invited to their family celebration (they did not participate in the public one) and were really welcome. It was good for Ruthie to be with other children.

Until your next letter, and information of all your doings

Your loving Pappa

That time in my memory ...

I had a spending allowance of five dollars a week, with additional money banked every month as my "emergency allowance." That was a huge sum in those days. Out of it came incidentals for school and lunches, everything else was taken care of by my foster parents, who were most generous. So were all their relatives who never failed to present me with something they considered useful in my new life. It was mostly books that would help me with my English. There was the young people's edition of Shakespeare and the beloved Nancy Drew mysteries. I must admit, I read far into the night in the bathroom, since all lights had to be out when Aunt Grace went to bed. It was the one thing I didn't like about sharing a room, the lights-out policy. I was a voracious reader and never seemed to have enough time. I do remember, one "faked" illness, to get out of school in order to finish a book. Dr. Joe, being the wise doctor he was, ordered complete bed rest and the missing of a birthday party until all the bugs were gone. I learned a good lesson in fakery from that.

Letter from Ruth

April 15, 1935

Dear Big Sister Thea,

How do you like my English script? Isn't it neat? I like hearing about all the things you get especially the clothes. Your Easter outfit sounds really great, particularly the sailor hat with violets on it. I got a pair of new shoes for Pesach[2], and I paid for most of them myself. I have a savings bank, which counts every penny and doesn't open up until it reaches 5 Marks. Then it automatically springs open, but the minute you put another coin in, it closes up again for the next 5 Marks, so I start all over again. This time I am saving for a camera. We had a wonderful time at the Kempf confirmation. All the family was there, no outsiders. They did not go to the community confirmation celebration, because they could not invite us. They are good friends.

Your girlfriends, even those who are in the BDM[3], say you must write more often how wonderful it is to be in America. Some wish they were Jewish so they could go. I have to close now since I have to help with the Pesach cleaning. You know how fussy Mama is about every crumb of *Chomitz*[4]. Mama is going to make matzo bundles for the neighbors and we will get our Easter eggs in exchange.

Love and kisses, your sister, Ruth

A word about my younger sister Ruth: she was too young to be signed up for the transport, and thus remained with my parents in Germany. She was a feisty little girl, always admonishing me as to my duty to relatives and friends. She was terrified to go to bed at night in the old nursery and could think of a hundred reasons for delaying this event, including the appearance of mice and monsters. Her Betty Boop and Minnie Mouse pajamas helped her overcome her nightly dramatics.

The claim to being Jewish by some of the Christian children should not be taken lightly. In my euphoric state of glowing letters, I can now see where their own futures seemed limited and uncertain.

---

2.   Passover
3.   *Bund Deutscher Mädchen,* the official organization for German girls.
4.   Any bread or unacceptable product for Passover.

One of the endearing customs in my childhood was the exchange of Easter Eggs for Matzoh. It always took place on Monday and usually involved 8-10 neighbors. There were no such exchanges here. Except for going to the relatives in River Forest for a sumptuous Seder, I do not remember Matzohs in the house.

We did have a lovely Easter celebration with Aunt Grace's relatives who came from Pittsburgh, instead of our going there. On Easter Sunday, we paraded up Michigan Ave. in our Easter finery to the Drake Hotel where they were staying. Michigan Avenue was the Chicago equivalent of New York's Park Avenue. On Easter Sunday, the fashionable of Chicago turned out in their Easter finery. I have also known it to be cancelled by howling snowstorms. As magnificent as these parades were, I was more impressed by the Chicago water towers, which reminded me of European castles. I accompanied the family to church, where the age-old ritual impressed me as an opera production would. I was full of reverence at the magnificent ceremony, which I had never seen in our modest European churches. Then, too, I was always in awe of Aunt Grace's brother, who wore an impressive gold watch, which he continually checked for time almost automatically; after all, he was in the railroad business. He was a courtly gentleman who always brought flowers whenever he came to visit, and this occasion was no exception. I received a bouquet of violets, my favorites, and felt very grown up indeed.

April 23, 1935

Dear Little Thea,

We are quite upset with the news that you have been moved to a new home and are no longer with the Sonnenscheins. What has happened? We are assuming it isn't something you did or that something happened to one of the family. I will try to call by telephone, but it is very difficult to make connections without running into censorship. We had not heard anything from the relatives about it either, so it must have been very sudden. Please let us know the circumstances as soon as possible. We are most anxious to hear.

How did you celebrate Seder? How do American matzos taste? Ours came from France (through Uncle Herman). All the good pieces of Christmas Goose preserved in fat in those stone crocks made a real feast. Over the holiday, we had a house full of relatives and that is good. They like coming here and enjoy Mamma's hospitality. We also had Easter with our Christian neighbors and that has not changed. We know who our friends are and that is comforting. The rest we leave alone. We had lots of Easter eggs and fish from the neighbors, and lamb from a customer in Lautersheim. People are still kind and caring.

So you see: Life goes on. Children are born and the old ones die, that is something the Nazi laws cannot regulate.

So, please, please let us know what has happened to account for your change in homes. We pray it is nothing that was your fault.

Your anxious Pappa and the family

That time in my memory ...

My leaving the Sonnenschein seemed like a shock at first hearing, but it was done with only love and understanding by generous people who saw in their age a handicap in raising an active child, waiting to challenge the world. They felt a younger family, with children, would give me a greater advantage toward that projected future. It was an amiable parting, with contacts that lasted until their deaths.

The change in my life came right after the Easter holidays. I called Pappa immediately. I was so shocked, but with Aunt Grace's and Uncle Joe's assurance that nothing with change in their affection for me, I accepted the fact that they were just too old for a growing young child and that their own somewhat sedentary lifestyle was too confining for me. The committee had found a lovely younger family with children in the suburbs of Chicago, where I could roam freely to satisfy my curiosity.

Aunt Lydia and Uncle Ernest came to pick me up and I remember all the things I had to take with me. My wardrobe no longer fit into the suitcases I brought with me, so there was a new set of luggage and a case for all my books. I took the Shirley Temple Doll to give to my new little sister, and I insisted on stopping at Marshall Fields to buy my new little brother a gift. What do you buy for a three year old boy? We settled on a spotted stuffed horse.

The next day, Aunt Lydia and Uncle Ernest took me to Winnetka where the address we were given was that of one of the loveliest estates I had ever seen. It reminded me of a picture I once saw of an English garden by the sea. The house was oak beamed and stretched along a white stone driveway glistening in the sun. The soft colors of spring were everywhere and we could hear Lake Michigan roaring in the background. I cannot describe my feelings. Why was I so lucky? I could hear Aunt Lydia in the background questioning my uncle over and over again, "Are you sure this is it? Look at the address again. Are you sure?" As we approached the front door, it opened and two bouncing children tumbled out: a sturdy seven year old girl with a shy smile and an excited three year old boy, grinning from ear to ear. They were to be my new sister and brother, Betty Ann and Larry. Behind them came a handsome lady, trying to calm them down. That was Anne Perlstein, who was to be known from then on as Aunt Anne. My aunt and uncle made the introduction and I followed in a daze. Aunt Anne clasped me in her arms and I was so happy I understood her English welcome. Uncle Harry, her husband, I would meet at dinnertime. I remembered my European upbringing and made a Knickschen (a curtsey) as I presented a bouquet of flowers to Aunt Anne. With this little ceremony, the children became quiet, solemn and big-eyed, as they took in whole scene. We entered the house with overlapping conversation, everyone talking at once. By now, the children were hanging on both of my hands, and as I said before, I was in a complete daze, gorging myself on sights and sounds.

How can I describe the house? The outside was an estate like an English manor house. The inside was as lovely as the outside, large like a castle, but so comfortable and inviting, as a real home should be. A winding staircase in a turreted tower made the castle picture complete. We went to the dining room, overlooking an already greening garden, sloping down to the lake. A young woman met us there, and she was introduced as Tagne, the children's nursemaid. She was Finnish. Since I was too old to have a nanny, I was told she would be my friend, but that she would still govern the "children's domain." Over ice cream and cake we talked about everything that focused around me up to now. What would be from now on, I dared not guess. All I remember is that soft firm voice assuring me that everything would be fine and how happy *they were to have me. The children became restless, and anxious to show me their world. Tagne took them away to make sure their rooms were tidy for my "inspection."*

We said goodbye to my aunt and uncle who seemed much relieved with the change in my circumstances. After they left, Aunt Anne put her arm around me and took me to the library, where I saw more books than even Pappa had. There were beautiful paintings, which later I could identify as Winslow Homer, a Grant Woods, a George Bellows, and a statue replica of the famous Michelangelo David. She explained again that Uncle Harry would join us at dinner, as he traveled from his office in the city everyday. He would be picked up at the railroad station. She then took me to an enormous kitchen, where I met the staff, a virtual international colony: Mrs. Darnell was an Irish cook; Arnold, the chauffeur was a butler, man of all supervisory work, and a one time Chicago policeman; his wife, Karin, was the upstairs maid, sometimes waitress, and came from Sweden; the cook's helpers and Mr. Philbean, the gardener, were from the area. They were the essence of the household who would all do their best to help me become part of the family. I was still shy and speechless, but shook hands with everyone. Aunt Anne explained that although they were there to make my life comfortable, it was up to me to lend a helping hand wherever I could. Mrs. Darnell would show me anything in the kitchen, including how to cook.

She then showed me all through the house, after which I was free to stay in my room until dinnertime, when I was to meet Uncle Harry. So this was to be my new home and family, for how many years to come, I could only guess.

7

May 1935

HEADLINES OF THE DAY:

PARIS—France, U.S.S.R. Sign Pact of Mutual Assistance

GERMANY—Defying Treaty ban, Germany Fortifies Schleswig Province

WASHINGTON—National Recovery Administration to Close Down as Works Progress Administration Begins Work

LONDON—Britain to Triple Air Forces by 1938

PRAGUE—Russia Agrees to Protect Czechoslovakia from Invasion

May 5, 1935

Dearest Little Thea,

We were so relieved and delighted with your call from Winnetka that I must write you this very evening and mail the letter, yet, tonight. Although we did not understand word for word what Mr. And Mrs. Perlstein tried to tell us about you coming to live with their family, we know they are so happy you joined them and their children. It sounds too good to be true that you should be so fortunate as to have two caring families as your sponsors. That the Sonnenscheins felt you should be with a younger family with children is understandable, they only see you less lonely and more active and I thank them for their observation. Giving you a goodbye party with all their relatives downtown (now I know what Downtown is) is touching and loving. That they will keep in touch with you is also reassuring. We understand that it is another whole new phase of your life in new surroundings: (The house sounds unbelievable, as you describe it, *wie ein Schloss*[1]), a new school, and all kinds of lessons. I hope you can fulfill some of their hopes for you, as you are well on the way of doing.

Again we await your description of your new life and all you do.

With much love—Your Pappa

That time in my memory ...

Harris and Anne Agazim Perlstein were in their late thirties or early forties. They had two adopted children: a girl, 7 years old, Betty Ann, and a boy, Larry, 3 years of age. I was to be the older sister. The family lived on a lovely estate in Winnetka, Illinois and was in very comfortable circumstances. All of Winnetka, it seemed to me, was made up of homes of families in very comfortable circumstances—from estates by the lake to the individual wide-porched houses, sitting on well-groomed lawns on side streets—homes of people who had successful careers that provided the economic stability of the country. The Perlsteins had a lively household of servants: nursemaid, butler, maid, cook, chauffeur, gardener and yardman, and a plethora of dogs. There were activities of every kind; sports, outings, music, and family entertainment. There didn't seem to be enough time for everything I wanted to do. I loved it!

I was to start school the following week. Meanwhile, I explored the outdoors, which was so beautiful in the spring. There was a path to a small cove by the lake, which was to become a favorite of mine for reading and daydreaming. The weekend brought lots

---

1.   Like a castle

of friends and relatives of the family and again I was reticent and overwhelmed. I really felt the language handicap, as some of the children thought I "talked funny."

I already mentioned all the staff that surrounded the family and they were truly helpful in familiarizing me with the household. Arnold became my staunch supporter. I was still a little frightened of "Uncle Harry." He was such an impressive man in spite of his twinkling eyes and mild manners. Although the children overwhelmed him with hugs and kisses when he came home, I did not feel I could do so. The school I entered was Winnetka Elementary and Junior High School where I was put into my proper grade, the seventh. I also received speech lessons, reminding me now of Professor Henry Higgins, from the play "Pygmalion", as I tried to get rid of my guttural "Rs", "Ts" and "Ss". I was also enrolled into the Dushkin School of Music for piano and the Winnetka Fortnightly, where children were taught to dance, learn good manners, and become sociable creatures. Most important, I was taken to the dentist and although I had good teeth, a weekly visit was necessary to correct all the faults that were apparent, especially a re-alignment. Although braces are today an accepted feature, at that time they were pretty rare, and I hated them and their limitations on foods that I liked. No wonder I rarely smiled and wouldn't have my picture taken.

I couldn't brood about these shortcomings, though; there were too many things to see and do. I had a new bicycle, new friends, lessons of all kinds, including tennis from Uncle Harry, who was an excellent player and had a tennis party every Sunday morning when he wasn't away on business. I read ferociously, mostly adult magazines like the "New Yorker", and the "Delineator." Children's magazines didn't interest me, but anything about beautiful houses did. Once a month, Aunt Anne and I went downtown to shop and attend Dr. Frederick Stock's Symphony for Children. You might say he was the forerunner to Leonard Bernstein's Music for the Young People and a legend in symphonic history. What also endeared him to me was that, he had a German accent and twinkling eyes and a gallant manner like my grandfather had. That similarity endeared him even more as an influence in my young life and my passion for classical music.

May 13, 1935

Dearest Little Thea,

We just received your dear lines and hasten to answer them right away. We are so relieved that your new home is so welcoming and that you are adjusting so well to it. I am sure your adjustment to the new school will go equally well. From the description of the house and its surroundings, it sounds like a manor house in an English park. You won't have to go on any vacation. It sounds so beautiful with all the trees, the flowers and the sea close by.

Be careful when you ride your new bike, especially the hill you mentioned which sounds very steep. Pay attention to all the traffic regulations. Ruth also wants a bike, and we said when her legs get longer, we'll think about it. Although we are still in business, we must be very careful with all the regulations. Thank G-d for my loyal customers, mostly in the outlying farms and towns. They are more prompt in their payments than before, even though I tell them there is no hurry.

As you sit in your beautiful room, think of us and thank G-d for your luck. He is really watching over you and all of us. I know you will let "Uncle Harry" and "Aunt Anne" know how much you appreciate all they are doing for you. My hands are on your head in the age-old Priestly Blessing, 'May the Lord bless you and keep you. May the Lord grant you His Favor. May the Lord cause His Countenance to shine upon you, and give you peace. "Kein Ye-Hi Rat-son." [Translated from the Hebrew as 'So may it be Your will.']

Your loving Pappa

That time in my memory ...

This is the blessing that typifies my father and his intense religious concepts. He attributes all of his actions as the will of God. In his letters the word "God" is not fully written out, as was his custom: "G-tt" in German, or "G-d" in English.

I never considered Pappa as Orthodox, rather as a German liberal Jew, although many of his practices were much more conservative than those to which I was now exposed in Reform Judaism, with its Sunday services, a minimum of Hebrew, and confirmation, which I witnessed for the first time that June. There was one Reform congregation in Glencoe, Illinois, and its members came from all over the North Shore.

My bicycle became my pride and joy, and I was allowed to ride it to school on good days. I could even ride it up and down the steep hill that stretched upward from our house toward Tower Road. Thanks to Arnold, I learned to keep it in top shape. My companion on these joyous rides was a beautiful Great Dane, named Captain, my favorite of all the dogs. I considered him my guardian and in the aftermath of the Lindbergh kidnapping, he truly acted as such. He was so huge that the children were afraid of him, since he knocked them down when he wanted to play. They preferred a feisty little Scottie, who was not above nipping them in the ankles when he felt like it. I still have his nip marks on my ankle. My belief is that Captain died of a broken heart because the children shied away from him and his overwhelming strength. He was such a beautiful creature.

I always liked big dogs. I remember Mamma having a little big-eyed Chihuahua. She had a handmade collar and coat and Mamma adored her. She was always shivering and sniveling. At best, I tolerated her. As I said, I liked big dogs. Besides Captain, there was a Labrador retriever, but he never came into the house.

And of course there were the dogs and horses we kept on the farm northwest of Chicago. We visited there at least once a month. It was run by a resident manager and was always a hub of productive activity. Each of us had our own garden plot, and, moreover, we were responsible for the care of the animals, under the watchful and guiding eye of the stable manager.

Letter from Mamma:

May 27, 1935

Dearest Little Thea,

You are probably surprised to get such a long letter from me, but Pappa is still out of town writing immigration travel tickets and insurance papers. Thank goodness, that is still a going business. The store, even with Mrs. Kemp's fine management, is a losing business. Nobody makes beautiful dresses anymore. The men wear the terrible brown uniform and the women all peasant dresses, straw hats, and those black, red and green jackets. Of course, in Frankfurt and Berlin, there are satin gowns and jewels. I have sewn my jewelry in my dresses. You never know when they tell you to pack a suitcase for a "temporary" evacuation "to a safer place."

I am so glad you are out of all of this. I only wish that Ruth were. Perhaps the family that owns the candy business will still want her, but with her nightmares and sleeping problems, I am reluctant to let her go.

I hope you will have a good summer. It is very hot for May and there are lots of storms and floods. One of the children at the mill drowned. You remember, the sister in your class died of tuberculosis and all of you children sang at her funeral. You don't have to be Jewish to have a sad life. I try to remember that as events bear down on us.

Please call the Chicago relatives. When you don't contact them, they get mad at us. We still hope they will send us the papers as we must get out of here.

Pappa would not like me to write so pessimistically—we still have many good moments of family holidays with good food, good music, our books and the quiet walks in the woods. And, then, of course, there are your letters: they keep hope alive! As always, I close with warm embraces,

Your loving Mamma

That time in my memory ...

As I've mentioned before, the transformation in my mother had been remarkable. As her social life shrank, her interest in home and family took on new dimensions. At the time of my arrival in the U.S. many families became interested in adopting a refugee child. Sad to say, that interest slackened as the need became greater. The family that was interested in Ruth had a thriving candy business with outlets in well-established department stores all over the Midwest. Although, it would have been wonderful for Ruth, Mamma was still reluctant to let her go because of her sleeping problems. As the interest in these refugee children waned, so did the family's interest in my sister. I dreaded to tell Mamma about it. I was also caught in the cross fire as far as the Chicago relatives were concerned. With my full schedule of school and other activities, it became more difficult to stay in constant contact with them. And so, they complained hurtfully to my parents, which made it more painful for me.

As I participated in so many lovely cultural experiences, I became very aware how Mamma would have loved them. I started to send her autographed programs of these events, wishing she too could have enjoyed them. Although many schools lacked cultural outlets for their students, those in the suburbs enjoyed more exposure to them than most. Around Christmastime, there were more professional and amateur productions than ever at the high school and Northwestern University. I saw my first "Christmas Carol", the "Messiah", and Chicago Opera's offering of "Hansel and Gretel", which had begun my love of opera many years before in Frankfurt.

8

June 1935

HEADLINES OF THE DAY:

ROME—Mussolini Bars New York Times for Editorial Criticism of Italian Fascists

LONDON—Stanley Baldwin Replaces Ramsey MacDonald as Prime Minister

LONDON—Britain Offers German Reich 35% Increase in German Naval Fleet, 45 % in U-Boats

OMAHA—Martial Law declared in Wake of Strike Rioting

MOSCOW—100,000 Youths Demonstrate Readiness for Red Army Service

June 5, 1935

Dear Little Thea,

If this letter is a little later than usual, please forgive me. I have been traveling (again) to help the relatives and talk to families who also wish to send their children to the U.S.A.

In Heusweiler, in spite of the annexation of the Saar[1], business has not diminished, but the relatives in Homburg are ready to emigrate. As they are retired, it should be no great problem, except for Jenny who wants to go to Palestine. How many families must split to survive? The chaos this new law has caused in families, playing Christian relatives against their Jewish members, is indescribable. Almost every family we know is touched by it, including our own with Mama's relatives.

We're grateful that Cousin Max has stayed clear of "Aryan entanglements", and they cannot label him a *Rasenschänder* (Race Defiler). I find it remarkable that he was been able to keep his post as a sales representative.

But enough of my musing, you are too young to be concerned about such political shenanigans. We're anxious to hear about your summer plans. Does the entire family go on a holiday, or will you be going alone? You seem to be so busy with so many activities, but you must not forget your school work. Remember that is the primary reason you are there.

This week is *Shavuot*[2] and Mama is deep into cleaning. Thank God she still has some help. It is such a large house with the synagogue. We will again enjoy the company of the faithful believers who make up our far flung congregation and, of course, the visiting relatives. I shall do my utmost to give them a meaningful religious service.

Please keep peace in the family and write your Aunt and Elsie. The latter has a much easier job now as companion to an elderly lady. We are still waiting for a picture. It does not have to be a formal portrait. Any snapshot will do.

Fondly—Your Papa

---

1. The Versailles Treaty had removed the iron- and coal-rich Saar basin from German administration. In 1935 the annexation of the Saar territory was effected by means of a plebiscite of German residents, who voted to rejoin Germany.
2. An agricultural thanksgiving day in the spring that commemorates the giving of the Ten Commandments at Mt. Sinai.

That time in my memory ...

My half-sister Elisabeth, familiarly called "Elsie" had moved to Chicago to be nearer to me, although we did not have the opportunity to meet more than once a month. As I recall, the lack of attention by me always brought some level of tension to the situation, as the Chicago relatives tended to complain to Mama of my inattentiveness.

The reference to Rasenschänder is significant. It means one who shames the nobility of the German race, as the intermarriage between Christian and Jew. Hitler put this horrible designation on intermarried families and this affected many of our relatives. Strangely enough, it was not considered as outrageous for a Christian male to have a Jewish wife, as it was the other way around.

I continued to have reminders of my obligation to do well in school and to be grateful for all that was being done for me. It was always with me. I think it still motivates me today.

I remember an assembly of my classmates, and how I managed to keep all their interest in spite of my halting English for a fifteen minute talk about growing up in Germany. The questions at that time were most interesting, many still going back to the concept of the Hun of World War I. No one, including myself, realized that a much greater villain was looming in the wings.

With the help of my classmates, I finally got the hang of what it was to diagram a sentence. That was a bewildering problem since the day I entered school and didn't know what a sentence was, much less how to diagram it.

By now too, we were making plans for the summer. The family vacation was to be at Michiana Shores, and after that I was to go to camp in Wisconsin. Meanwhile, I settled in at school and the extra attention made me work all the harder. Music lessons occupied much of my time, and since I was impatient with my own halting pieces, I used to pretend it was I playing Liszt and Chopin on the piano rolls that were used in the music room. It was ambitious daydreaming. I was ecstatic when I graduated to "Fur Elise" and was to play a duet with my teacher, Miss Stahlin in an upcoming recital.

The sobering thoughts of Germany and all it held for my family seemed far away. At times I felt enormously guilty about Ruth in particular and resolved to send her another goodie package right away.

I could not resolve the apparent inconsistencies of my world: Here I was, growing up carefree with only the normal worries that a child should feel; yet, at the same time, I had to confront the adult world of politics and war. I felt the stabbing pain of anxiety every time I read a newspaper or received one of Pappa's letters detailing just how cruel and capricious people could be to one another.

June 15, 1935

Dear Daughter,

This time your letter arrived in record time, and I will reply to it just as speedily. It is always good to hear that you are enjoying your new family, your school and all the other activities. It has been unusually hot for this early in the summer, and Ruth has been spending most of her day swimming in the old *Klebsand*[3] swimming hole. I must say, for an artificially created hole, it fits the bill of lake very nicely, since it does have some shade trees and flowers around it. Do you remember how proud we all were when you proved you could swim across it and then were towed back by the lifeguard in a huge red rubber ring? Your classmates stopped scoffing at you as a non-swimmer and called you a champion.

You speak of getting a riding habit, so I'm assuming you do horseback riding, or is it some other animal's back you climb on? Please send us a picture, I cannot imagine you grooming a horse—you who didn't even like to brush your own hair—that I would like to see. Perhaps you too could be in the picture, and then we would have one of you at the same time, as you are reluctant to have a separate one taken.

You still did not say what you are going to do during your vacation, which is so much longer than our children have. About your grades, again I must assume you received a report card, or do you only get it at Easter? So many questions, I know, but it's only because your life is so different there. There is so much more to keep track of. What you read, what you learn, what you wear, and what you eat: all of these may seem simple, but they are very important to us at the same time.

You mentioned a Temple. Again, I assume you mean a synagogue and that there is "Sunday School" for boys and girls together, that you will be confirmed in a few years, and that you are beginning to study for it now. What about *Bar Mitzvah*? Is there such a thing in the U.S. temples?

Summer will be here soon and we will begin helping the relatives with harvesting. It is good to be on the land and close to nature, where there is a sense of reality and beauty.

Write soon—Your loving Pappa

---

3. Type of sand or clay with minerals that are used in producing tile.

That time in my memory ...

One of the sports to which I became attached was horseback riding. The Perlsteins had a tenanted farm outside of Chicago with farm animals in abundance. I immediately took to the horses and fell in love with one called "Rolli", hence the complete riding outfit. The reference to pictures of the horse, possibly with me in it, was Dad's way of reminding me that I had not sent many pictures. The reference to the Temple rather than synagogue was that the Perlstein family practiced Reform Judaism as opposed to Traditional or Orthodox. The rite of confirmation had supplanted the traditional "Bar Mitzvah" and usually took place at the age of fourteen. Although confirmation was still a year away, as an outstanding student of the confirmation class, I was given the Flower Address to compose and present. This was a very distinct honor. Although I had many Jewish friends, many of my classmates and certainly my "Fortnightly" companions were not. I felt no discrimination, if there was, I was not aware of it. I know there were some of the suburbs where country clubs didn't welcome Jews, but then we had our own exclusive ones. Even among the Jews themselves you had discrimination between those who were descendants from Eastern Jewry opposed to those from Western Europe. As an example, one had formed the Standard Club and the other the Covenant Club. Uncle Harry belonged to both and our welcome at both of them was always warm and receptive. It was interesting to note, that even second generation American Jews still made the distinction between the Sephardic and the Ashkenazi tribes of Jews.

An exciting event at this time was the arrival of friends on the maiden voyage of the great liner, S.S. Normandie. We couldn't wait to welcome them and the souvenirs we were promised. I made up my mind, then and there, when I grew up I would sail the world in nothing but luxury liners.

Little did I know of what was ahead of me in living around the world! As a military wife and tourist, I have sailed on everything from Army transports to the last voyage of the S.S. United States when, as an Army wife, I returned with my family from our last military assignment in Europe.

June 24, 1935

Dearest little daughter,

If this seems a short letter, please forgive me, but I am going on another trip out of town at the suggestion of my good friends who know so much more of what is going on than I do. We are still in excellent health, which we hope you are too, in spite of all your dentist visits. Just remember what a beautiful smile you will have when it's all finished. With your vacation already started, you must have received your end-of-semester grades. No doubt, they are excellent, and you will send us a copy.

It is unseasonably hot here, and Ruth is at the lake every day. We, of course, take advantage of our cool bathtub, as we are no longer able to join the lake-goers. It is the equivalent of "Jews and dogs stay off the lawn", as you have mentioned also happens in the U.S.A.

You are going some place called Michiana Shores in Indiana for part of your vacation. It sounds wonderful; you can stay in the water all day. Be careful! You know you burn (and freckle) very easily. How long will you be there, as you also spoke of going to camp? Please write us the address, so we can write you there. Surely, you can let us have some pictures of you in these places.

Your friend, Elfriede, is still here, although her sister, who got her papers later, has left. It is a question about a health clearance, as she had pneumonia once, and they thought it was tuberculosis. Thanks to G-d you had no such problems! Gerda will be here for some of the summer and take Ruth to Bremen with her. That way, the little one, too, can have a vacation.

We will be sending you some books, as now they search for decadent literature, as well as "degenerate" works of art. Book burnings have also been dramatic events like Wagner operas, but far more dangerous to the spirit of free thought. The music of Mendelssohn, one of the greatest German composers, cannot be played, nor do the German people read the beautiful and expressive poems of Heinrich Heine anymore. Where will all this nonsense end?

In Haste—Your devoted Pappa

That time in my memory ...

"Degenerate art" had become the banner under which the Third Reich persecuted painters, writers, and composers, either because they were non-Aryan (Heine, Mendelssohn, Chagall) or their ideas were too modernistic for the very conventional Nazi regime (Thomas Mann, Hindemith, Klee). Some of the giants in those arts were so

labeled, and their work was forbidden in Germany. Ironically, the exhibits of "degenerate art" drew more public viewing than any exhibits in the past. An actual war existed between Göring and Göbbels, as well as other high ranking Nazis, for the possession of these works—which were highly prized and whose possession was very lucrative, whether approved by Hitler or not. As Pappa mentioned, book burning became the order of the day. It took on the pageantry of a Wagnerian opera, as did most rallies. Göbbels was an expert at staging public displays of near-hysterical patriotism.

As for my part here, I continued to be exposed to culturally everything possible in a rich variety. With so many of Aunt Anne and Uncle Harry's friends' children going to Northwestern, we could participate in many family activities at the university. At Northwestern University, I saw my first college revue, my first collegiate football game, and a lecture on contemporary American English by Professor Bergen Evans. Later, Prof. Evans became a particular favorite of mine with his enormous knowledge of the English language. Of course, there were my weekend visits to downtown Chicago, and the movies Uncle and Aunt rented to help me with my English. Learning was such a rich tapestry of sights and sounds—Europe and its cultural decline seemed far away, because this new world was so rich in learning opportunities for a young and eager mind.

9

July 1935

HEADLINES OF THE DAY:

NEW YORK—100,000 Welfare Recipients Get Jobs under Newly Created PWA

GERMANY—Germany Announces Construction of Two New Battleships, 28 U-Boats

NEW YORK—Local Communists Raid German Liner "Bremen"; Throw Swastika into the Hudson River

BERLIN—Nazi repression of Jews is Intensified

ADDIS ABABA—Emperor Haile Selassie Rejects Italian Sphere of Influence in Ethiopia, Vows to Fight Invasion to Last Man

July 4, 1935

Dear little Thea,

Your last few letters were slow in coming, so I want to answer them immediately. Do not worry too much about what you read in the newspapers. The new laws spring up like weeds every day. The ambitious all want their say. They now have decided if only one of your grandparents was Jewish, you are a *Mischling*[1], as Mamma was, and cannot be governed by the rules for full-blooded Jews. They deplore the Jewish cowardice in World War I and then sent your Great Uncle the Iron Cross First Class for your Uncle Gustav, who flew with von Richthofen[2]. He sent it back, since officially, it was "unmerited by a Jew." He wrote he assumed it had been sent to him in error. We are all very proud of him.

This is a special day for the United States, and I'm sure you will be celebrating it festively. I hope by the next one, we can join you in such a celebration.

We are pleased that you fit into school so nicely. No doubt you will get good grades before you leave for summer vacation. You must be patient with your English. That Aunt Anne has special lessons to get rid of your German accent is very encouraging, but in time you will speak like all the other Winnetka children. The "Fortnightly Dance Class" sounds like much fun and a wonderful way to be with other boys and girls your age. As I said before, when you are finished with the dentist, you will have a beautiful smile, and one day will be very grateful. I wish our children here had better care for their teeth. There is only one dentist we may visit, and he's in Frankenthal.

We have constant visitors, and that is good for Mamma. She doesn't feel so socially cut-off with everybody, and besides she beats everyone in *Skat*[3].

My old clients are slowly dying away. That grand lady, Frau von Muller, who was such a special friend, is the latest to be buried. Yet we still have others who are loyal and survive day by day. I cannot ask for more than the friendship of those who will never change their allegiance.

Let us hear about your vacation. You said you might go to camp. In Germany, the word "camp" today is a very chilling word, as it can mean anything from labor camp to concentration camp—none of them bode any good for our

---

1.   Child of a mixed Jewish and Christian marriage.
2.   Manfred von Richthofen, the German flying ace of World War I, commonly called "The Red Baron." Mamma had six brothers who fought in World War I—on both sides, the French and the German.
3.   Three-hand card game

people. Be careful riding your bike, especially on the big hill you keep mention-
ing as a challenge.

With warmest greeting to the Perlstein family, it's nice you have a little brother
and sister to care for.

Your devoted Pappa

That time in my memory ...

*One of the reasons that I didn't like my picture taken was because of the terrible braces
that I had to wear on my teeth. The dental work I needed was extensive after all, as
very little had been done in Germany.*

*Pappa's reference to "camp" reflects the growing number of concentrated barracks
for forced labor in Germany. There was not yet any reference to Jewish concentration
camps; they came later during the War. Nevertheless, it was becoming commonplace
for ordinary Germans—whether because of political unreliability or affiliation, or
because of general "undesirability"—to be removed to camps, which were variously
called "relocation centers", "re-education centers", or some other seemingly innocuous
term.*

*But no one was fooled. The Nazi Government, when it removed individuals to
these camps, did not advertise the fact. And even the most fearless Germans dared not
ask the most telling questions: "Where are they?"; "Who have you taken?"; and, the
most frightening question of all, "Why?"*

*Camp Burr Oaks in Wisconsin was a delightful place where I spent the rest of the
summer. It drew girls from all over the United States as fellow camp-mates. I had no
lack of invitations to visit them on vacation. The girls were all from well-to-do families from as far away as Texas to Maine. The directors were Mr. and Mrs. Rice from
Evanston, who made a point of meeting with the campers and parents in various cities
around the United States during the winter months. We were to be housed in log cab-
ins, (but with amenities such as showers, baths and house mothers). The housemothers
were teachers from private and public schools from the Illinois and Wisconsin area.
Specialists, like the riding master, archery teacher, drama and singing coaches, came
from institutions all over the United States. We had blue uniforms for the week and
white for Saturday and Sunday, all provided by Marshall Fields. Interestingly enough
we kept the Sabbath. After a short morning service there were no strenuous activities
on both Saturday and Sunday. They were mostly devoted to the arts and music. Meals
were nourishing with emphasis on chicken, fish and local vegetables. The rule was you*

must clean your plate before you leave the dining room. I hated liver, but fortunately there was a girl who liked it and I made a deal with her—her fish for my liver. It worked out great. We learned to hide some of the uneaten food in handkerchiefs under our belts which were about 2 inches wide—what we could have done with baggies in those days!!

July 15, 1935

Dear Little Thea,

I don't need to be reminded that this is just before your birthday. We know you'll be celebrating in great style. You see you don't have to go to Hollywood to have a wonderful life. You can make it so wherever you are. We are so happy that you can describe everything that is happening so beautifully; it means so much to us. Perhaps you should be a writer instead of a doctor, as Gerda and Wolfgang planned for your future. That of course is all old history, since they are no longer together, and she must find other ways to get her medical career back on track. Although she is with lovely people, she is very lonely in Bremen, and anxious to leave the country.

Your 4th of July celebration sounded wonderful. A real American holiday!! The country club where the Perlsteins celebrated with their friends sounds like another world from that we live in, and fireworks—Ruth would give anything to see fireworks. They have some along with the torchlight parades for all the big Nazi events, but naturally we are excluded from all that. When I think of all the Jews who thought Hitler would do something good for them, I could laugh if it wasn't so tragic. So much has happened even since you left, and it gets worse every day! I am so fortunate to have the good friends and relatives I have here and out of town. You notice I am out of town quite a lot, whenever a "propaganda event" is on the horizon.

But enough of my gloom and doom. For us, it is a blessing you're out of it. The Perlsteins must be very pleased with your report card—I wish I could communicate my gratitude better, but I rely on you to do so for me. You mention important people coming to the house; that must mean Mr. Perlstein must be important, too. I have never asked what he does for a living. Obviously it is something that permits the family to live well. The main thing is they are good people and take good care of you.

For your birthday, we send you much love and blessings.

Your loving family and Pappa.

That time in my memory ...

I have mentioned before that my foster family was well-to-do. Harris Perlstein was President and Chairman of the Board of the Pabst Blue Ribbon Brewing Company. He was on the boards of many charitable organizations, both here and abroad, and at various universities around the country. An affable and astute man, Harris Perlstein had friends who ranked high in industry, government, and in the sports and enter-tainment world. He was then as he would be now: an exemplary role model for a young and impressionable would-be American.

Anne Agazim Perlstein was his perfect partner, foremost as a mother, excellent hostess, and a no-nonsense businesswoman. Her simplicity in a world full of so much sham and pretense was a wonderful example to me.

Like all children, Betty Ann and Larry Perlstein engaged me in sibling rivalry, which always ended in hugs and "I love you's" after the battle. I was the older sister and therefore staked my claim as such. Both children were adopted and in the heat of one of those battles, Betty Ann let me know they were real adoptees, while I was only temporary. In my most dignified and haughty hands-on-the-hips stance, I sniffed "but I know my real parents." With that they began to sob and cry horribly, rushed to their mother's bedroom, and between hiccupping sobs claimed that I had called them orphans. This of course was immediately disclaimed by Aunt Anne, who gathered all of us on her bed, and soothed us with the well-known quote, "You're all our children, one as dear as the other," and that we were all hand-picked. A lot of parents had to take what came to them. Nothing was ever said about it again, and peace reigned once more.

As to my first Fourth of July, it was everything the Fourth of July should be, with straw hats and banners, and a barbeque picnic at the club pool. There was a puppet show for the children, a tennis tournament, and the movie musical for the grown-ups. When it got dark, there were fireworks that lit up the sky in red, white and blue. A small combo provided music for dancing, and I wished I were sixteen years old so I could dance with the adults instead of hopping around the grass with the children. I still stumbled a little when reciting the Pledge of Allegiance to my new country. "Indi-visible" gave me a lot of trouble and I finally learned the correct expression was "for which it stands" instead of "for witches dance."

Strangely enough, I felt no split loyalties. Much as I missed my parents, I could only hope that some day I would hear them too say the Pledge of Allegiance. I was very opti-mistic about it.

July 25, 1935

Dear little daughter,

Although we had no letters this past week, we are so happy to receive two, plus the one from Mrs. Perlstein. We're assuming you have gone to camp (as Mrs. Perlstein writes) and that is the cause for the interruption in our communication. We know you must be all right, and, as always, very busy. School vacation has started here, and we're not quite sure where we are sending Ruth, possibly to Aunt Delphine. Max will be here again at the end of the week. Last weekend, we all went to the funeral of dear cousin Ruth, who finally is at rest after suffering so long. I sometimes envy those who pass away to eternal rest and are spared the suffering to come.

The note from Mrs. Perlstein was a welcome blessing. Miss Schmidt translated it for us. That way we also know its contents will be all over town. She says you call them Aunt Anne and Uncle Harry. It goes the same for all their many relatives, and that Betty Ann and Larry are truly like a little sister and brother, and that you are a good example for them. You can translate my letter to them, I am sure.

We hope the next mail will bring letters from your camp and how you spent your birthday. I also hope it has a good wish for Mamma's birthday. You know she is only a few days after you. I fervently wish I could tell her we have the exit papers. That would be a real birthday present for her. Like Job and Lazarus, we must be patient: therein lies our strength.

With love and G-d's blessings—Your Pappa

That time in my memory ...

My birthday was a family celebration at the North Shore Country Club. Although it was exclusively Jewish, it had all the amenities of any other well-to-do country club. One additional feature was the festive meals on the Jewish holidays. It did not adhere to strict dietary laws, so I felt perfectly comfortable having a hot dog and a chocolate milkshake at the same time. I will admit that I was sad that Mamma's birthday could not be celebrated at the same time. Aunt Anne thought we should send Mamma a summer stole which we picked out on one of our trips to downtown Chicago. School had been out since June and we had spent 2 weeks at Michiana Shores. My report card was very good which of course pleased my foster parents. The big plus was that I was catching up in English. My knowledge of Europe was another plus in my

Geography class. I had to explain to Pappa that here grades were recorded as A, B, C, D & F—F being failure.

I was in love with the movies and aside from the classics which the family showed, twice a month I was allowed to go with my friends to Evanston for a Saturday treat. My accent continued to be very German in spite of the exposure to good English and my diction lessons.

Meanwhile, I was being outfitted for Camp Burr-Oaks where I was to spend the rest of the summer. What a carefree, uncomplicated summer I spent in Wisconsin while the storm clouds of war gathered over Europe. I must admit I was scarcely aware of them, even though I faithfully read Colonel McCormick's conservative Chicago Tribune. I was more interested in the comics and radio serials than the ominous political reports from over there. Nevertheless, my anxieties were always present, even if they had not totally absorbed my thoughts.

10

August 1935

HEADLINES OF THE DAY:

WASHINGTON—18,000 Musicians to Receive Jobs in Federal Arts Relief Program

ITALY—Mussolini Calls Up 300,000 Troops

LONDON—Baldwin Announces Government is Prepared to Let Italy Take Land in Ethiopia

PARIS—Mediation Talks Fail, as Italy Rejects Economic Concessions; Mussolini Demands Control of All of Ethiopia

ANCHORAGE—Will Rogers and Famed Aviator Wiley Post Die in Alaska Air Crash

BERLIN—American Eugenist Clarence Campbell Hails Nazi Racial Policies

WASHINGTON—FDR signs First Neutrality Act, Forbidding Arms Shipments to Nations at War

---

August 10, 1935

Dear little girl,

Your last letter before camp arrived, and your birthday sounded so exciting. So many people *die ganze Mishpocha*[1] (the whole family), aunts and uncles from all over, even from Milwaukee, where the family is in the beer business. You even have a grandfather again, old Mr. Agazim, your Aunt Anne's father. We are all so happy for you. Ruth loves the new stationery with your name and address. It is very elegant, she says. If we send a picture for your new heart locket, will you send us a new one of you? The books you got for your birthday should really help you with your English. I like to think that you will save them for Ruth, so that she can learn English when she comes. It was also very thoughtful of your new parents to have a birthday cake at your fortnightly dance lesson and give you a surprise party. *Sei getröstet*[2]. Braces on your teeth are not so bad, if it gives you a beautiful smile later on when you're grown up. Then you can have all the chewing gum and caramel you want.

You mentioned two very interesting gentlemen at your birthday party, people who visit the family very often. One we have heard about, as he is a famous comedian in the U.S.A.: Mr. Eddie Cantor. He is very funny, but his pictures can no longer play in Germany, as he is Jewish. Many artists, actors and musicians have left or are leaving here, because they are no longer allowed to carry on their art. That is so sad, as they have contributed so much to German culture. I predict a great loss to our culture that cannot be overlooked. On the other hand, they will contribute significantly to the American arts.

The other gentleman, whom you call "Uncle Ben", I do not know. You say he has a big dance orchestra in a night club, smokes a big cigar and teaches you new English words, like "Yowzah". He sounds very jolly and if he says you play the piano very well, I believe him. With a big band, he must be a good musician.

My dear child, I wonder if you know all the wonderful things you are exposed to. Absorb everything like a sponge, and you will have a full, rich life. In closing, I bless you with the three-fold blessing to you and your new family.

Your loving Pappa

---

1. German Yiddish for "the whole family"
2. German for "be comforted", one of Dad's much-used phrases

That time in my memory ...

I mentioned my birthday celebration, my 13th, in the last letter. It was particularly exciting, since Uncle Harry's friend Eddie Cantor, the actor and comedian, was in town and an invited guest. As a birthday present he sang his hit song from his show "Whoopie" to me. He was a charming and modest man, full of pride in his family—his wife Ida and his five daughters.

The gentleman whom I called "Uncle Ben" was another close friend of Uncle Harry's: Ben Bernie—a cigar-smoking bandleader who always answered his radio air-time introduction with "Yowzah, yowzah!" which he taught me to use as a greeting. "Uncle" Ben Bernie held forth at the Chez Paree Nightclub, which with its bevy of glamorous showgirls was the number one club in Chicago. Other Hollywood friends were Jimmy Durante and Groucho Marx. What continued to surprise me was that they were nothing like the characters they played on the stage and screen.

Since Uncle Harry's niece was in radio, many people from that side of show business also became familiar figures, the Ameche brothers for instance. So were the sports celebrities that were sponsored by the Pabst Brewing Company. A special favorite was Sid Luckman of the Chicago Bears. He "hired" my little brother Larry as a water boy for the team. I wished I could have been a cheerleader, but I was too young.

Among Uncle Harry's political friends were Presidential Advisor Bernard Baruch, former Governor Horner, the Chicago Democratic kingmaker Jacob Arvey, and Judge Julius Hoffman. Mr. Baruch was a particular favorite because, again, he reminded me of my grandfather. He was known to dispense advice from a White House park bench, and to me was one of the few politicos truly concerned about the situation in Europe. Jacob Arvey, known as the kingmaker, was another astute Chicago politician. Much later, he became the man behind Adlai Stevenson, a man I much admired. After WWII, Uncle Jack Arvey gave me his silver oak leaves (Lt. Col. Insignia) which I proudly pinned on my husband when he gained that rank years later. The outspoken Judge Julius Hoffman, of course, made his mark much later in the trials of the Chicago Seven. Governor Henry Horner had pretty much retired from the very active political scene due to ill health, but was still on the job in Springfield. Time away he spent at Deere Park, where children were always welcome. Meanwhile, there were also exchanges with Franklin D. Roosevelt, Henry Morgenthau and David Ben Gurion—men whom I admired but never met: All men who are part of the political heritage and history and the Twentieth Century.

At the time, the sports figures and politicians didn't interest me as greatly as the Hollywood stars. So, I once asked Uncle Harry, why didn't he sponsor leading men like Ronald Colman and Frederic March? I remember his gentle smile as he replied, "Honey, the people who cultivate these gentlemen don't drink my beer."

I became more aware of all the people around me, the contacts that provided me with such a positive outlook to the future. I only knew that life was much like the dreamland I had wished for, and that my reality was now sunny and pleasant, not harsh, as it seemed to be in my home-land. I did have sobering thoughts about my family, and what lay ahead for them; so teenage anxieties were always with me; but it only rarely entered my mind that I might not see my parents and sister again

August 20, 1935

Dearest Little Girl,

After a long wait, we finally received your first letter from Burr Oaks camp, and took great joy in the fact that you were having such a wonderful time. We hope you write us many more letters from there, since you will be there the entire month. We already feel we know your bunkmates; that is, the girls in your cabin. Naturally, with as many girls as you mention, you cannot know all of them, but it is good to know you are making many new friends from all over the United States. They certainly keep you busy with swimming, riding, and archery, which is a new sport for you. Remember how you used to sing "*Mit dem Pfeil und Bogen durch Gebirg und Taβ*" in your physical training class? Now you can really sing that song!

The chorus group and the players club also sound interesting. What play are you giving on Parents' Day? It is another world, isn't it? So far removed from what we know. To Ruth, it sounds like a fairy story. Again we ask you, please send us pictures. Are you still afraid to take your picture with your braces showing? It doesn't matter to us at all, you must know that. So we anxiously await your next letter and photographs.

Here, we are having a very hot and sultry summer. Ruth's vacation is almost over, but she had a good time visiting all the relatives and now that we have little Fred, Uncle Herman's grandson, with us, she is doubly happy with her new playmate. I have been in Heusweiler helping Uncle Hermann and his family get ready to move to Luxemburg, where they bought a country estate. Farming and husbandry are the only work they can do there, and it will keep the young people very busy. So many of them will emigrate there, awaiting the time that they can move abroad. With the Annweiler relatives leaving, only the Schwegenheimers and we shall be left. Thanks G-d for Max, who in his travels shuttles between his parents and us. As always, we are grateful for our good health.

I am constantly asked how you were able to leave so quickly. I can only say G-d let me see the need, and I followed my conscience and instincts. Try to write all the relatives. They live by news from you young people. Continue to lead your beautiful life and be a credit to us all.

Your devoted Pappa

---

3.   German song, "With the bow and arrow over hill and dale"

That time in my memory …

I never realized what a blessing the far-flung relatives were: the visiting back and forth made the monotony of my parents' lives so much more bearable. My cousin, Max Baer, unlike his namesake, was not a boxer. I am eternally grateful to him for looking after my parents and all the relatives as conscientiously as he did. His ability to shuttle them about in his sales routine made life more pleasant for them, as rail travel became more and more restricted. How he managed to hold on to his Aryan job has always been a mystery to me.

"With my bow and arrow, over hill and dale" was one of my exercise songs in gymnastics. Although in exercise class we only went through the motion, I could now enjoy the real sport with my own set of bow and arrows. Camp that summer was a wonderful experience for me since there were girls from all over the United States. I became very good in geography and made long range plans for vacations in Biloxi, Mississippi; New Orleans, Louisiana; and Omaha, Nebraska, not really understanding how far these cities were from my home.

Caring for the horse that was assigned to me heightened the sense of responsibility even more. On parent's day, I was very proud to show off my horsemanship to my adopted family—even more so since I won a red ribbon, second prize, in the riding competition.

The Hollywood revue we gave for the parents was the vehicle that would lead us all to stardom. The guest of honor at this event was a young boy soprano, named Bobby Breen, whose career in Hollywood was well underway. He was there to support one of our campers, who would be his co-star in an upcoming picture. We all thought she would be the next Shirley Temple, and treasured the autograph party her parents gave for the whole camp. Sad to say, after her debut, we never heard of her again. We never realized that fame could be so fleeting. Bobby Breen continued to climb as the boy soprano until he could no longer sing with his voice cracking into masculine maturity. Today his pictures are re-issues as "in" DVD features.

11

September 1935

HEADLINES OF THE DAY:

UNITED STATES—Senator Huey Long of Louisiana Assassinated by Political Opponent

GERMANY—Amid Parades and Pageantry, 7th Nazi Party Congress Opens in Nuremberg, Germany

NUREMBERG—Hitler Decrees New Laws Banning Jews from German Politics

BERLIN—German Reich Announces Plan to Buy Out All Jewish Firms

GENEVA—League of Nations Decides to Invoke Sanctions if Italy Resorts to War

WASHINGTON—Secretary of State Cordell Hull Apologizes to German Reich for New York Judge's Release of Communists in Liner "S.S. Bremen" Incident

September 1, 1935

Dear Little Thea,

Your last letter from your days at camp was really like a book. Apparently, Wisconsin is quite a way from Winnetka, so it was wonderful that the whole Perlstein family came to see you on Parents' Day. I am sure they were proud of you winning a red ribbon in riding and all the other activities you showed them. The singing around the campfire sounds so wonderful. Here, the bonfires and the singing of Nazi-inspired songs only puts fear in our hearts. The friendships you made will keep you warm in memories until you see the girls again. We thank you for the group picture, but we can't see much of you. You look smaller than the other girls in the picture.

Now you will be going back to school where new adventures await you. Do you realize it is almost a year since you left? Since then things here have worsened. My loyal customers are threatened with a cut-off of their "*Winter Hilfs-Werke*[1]" if they buy anything from me. On the other hand, the government magnanimously offers to buy out all the Jews. One doesn't know what to believe. I thank G-d for the agencies which I am allowed to keep. Ironically, most of the travelers and insurers are Jews who are leaving the country or insuring their property.

Please be in touch with the relatives. After all, we still hope to get our visas from them. At this point, do not ask the Perlsteins to underwrite our immigration; by taking you into their home and furthering your education, they have done more than enough for us already. We will try every other means first; that will be our last resort. I hope it will not come to that.

The September festivals are in full swing, but we are no longer involved. Sadly, they are no longer the carefree celebrations they once were. They are full of propaganda and ominous martial airs. Mamma hardly steps across the threshold. She says she has everything she wants at home. At last she has made peace with herself over the disappointment of people whom she thought were her friends.

With loving greeting to you and the entire family—Your Pappa

---

1.   Winter relief

That time in my memory ...

Camp was a lovely memory and a very broad experience in community living and cooperation. I enjoyed everything but the discipline regarding food left on the plate. Even the admonition "Children in Europe are starving" didn't help any. I still didn't like liver, and used to tuck it into a handkerchief and then under my belt when no one was available to trade. Oh, what I could have done with plastic storage baggies in those days!

Even though Pappa writes that, "Thank G-d, we are all physically well", I could feel a sense of anxiety growing, since all of their efforts to emigrate speedily were being stymied at every turn by the demanding German regime. Pappa's request not to involve the Perlsteins in supplying visa certification for them was again noted, but with apprehension. At this time, I felt assured though that my uncles had it all under control.

Winter Hilfs-Werke was the German winter relief that helped farmers through the harsh winter times, with donations of food, coal, money, and warm clothing. All of these items could not be procured from Jews, with the threat of having such critical Government aid cut off.

Being in constant touch with the relatives became somewhat a bone of contention. I felt guilty about all of the great things that were happening to me, knowing that my cousins alternately were pleased or resented it. We invited my aunt's entire family for dinner on my return from camp, and, although it was done in Aunt Anne's gracious hospitable manner of putting everyone at ease—I felt stiff and painfully self-conscious. My cousins accused me of "showing off." Uncle Ernest seemed to be the only one truly relaxed—sharing jokes with Uncle Harry. The dinner and taking pictures seemed to relax everyone a bit more and presenting Aunt Lydia with a pillow I had embroidered at camp finally made the evening a success. I promised to visit them for the high holidays and celebrate with them. I would have to have special permission to leave school, as there was no automatic excuse for religious holidays, certainly not in North Shore schools. That came much, much later.

September 8, 1935

Dearest Little Thea,

Now that you are back from your wonderful vacation at camp, you must be refreshed and ready to tackle your school work again with new energies. You mention all the wonderful things that you did at camp: sports, music, painting, and building; it sounds like every hour of the day was taken. I hope you used your free time to read quietly and write down your thoughts. Remember the thoughtful quiet moments: They will be very valuable in your future.

All our summer company has left, and it is quiet once more. Uncle Herman picked up his little grandson, Fred, who loved it here, particularly when I took him fishing and he caught one. Yesterday, a huge package of food arrived from Uncle Herman's "*Gut*" (a farm estate) in Luxemburg, so we will not hunger for a long time. With the canning and preserving of fruits and vegetables by Mamma and Lenchen, we should be set for fall and winter. We in the country have the advantage over the city Jews who must buy every scrap of food. G-d has been good to us and we continue to trust in His grace. Certainly, that He has shown His Goodness to you has made our lot lighter and more hopeful. Continue to be a good daughter to your foster parents and bring them joy. Our only regret is we couldn't send Ruth with you, but very few children are leaving just now. Sad to say, the people in the U.S. are not as interested in sponsoring as they once were, and yet the need is greater than before. The little Stiefel boy is happy in the U.S.A., and so, one by one, they do get to leave, even if only in a trickle.

There is very little social life for Mamma, who loved all the entertaining she did, but now that she runs the house herself, she takes great pride in it. Her phonograph and classic records are her great joy and comfort.

I close with much love and begging for more pictures.

Your devoted, Pappa

That time in my memory …

My father's remarks give some insight into the problems faced by Jews all over Germany. Whereas city Jews could only purchase food under the baleful eye of the Nazi regime, Jews in the country, like my family, could find ways to survive, with the bounty of harvest all around them. The farm in Luxemburg also became home for Pappa's other brother, Benny, and his family.

Here in America, people were not as interested in bringing the young children out, although the need became more urgent. I still hoped to get a family to adopt Ruth, although Mamma was still hesitant about letting her go.

I could not picture Mamma without a busy social life, but that was the inevitable result of the ever-more restrictive measures. There were no more big parties or country festivals. The families rallied around the religious holidays and the birth and death cycles. There, you could still find the communication between the Jews and the Christians intact, since so many had relatives on both sides.

I was getting ready to enter another school year. I still had a lot of extra activities almost every day, although my voice lessons switched to Winnetka instead of downtown Chicago. There was talk of moving to Highland Park, but I felt sure I would be able to graduate 8ᵗʰ grade from Winnetka. I really did not want another school change, to have to establish myself all over again and make new friends. I asked Arnold, my confidant, but he only shrugged his shoulders and dismissed it as another rumor. Besides that he would drive me every day if it became necessary. Strange, as much as I loved Aunt Anne and Uncle Harry, it was Arnold and Karin, his wife, who were truly my confidants. It was to Karin and my sister Gerda I could talk about my puberty and the physical changes in my body. It was Karin who soothed me through my first menstrual period and my "heartbreak" over this boy or that one. I still found so many things to do, so much to learn, that kept me from lingering over my adolescent disappointments

Letter from Gerda

September 8, 1935

Dear Little Sister,

You're almost too big to call little sister any more. Although I should be angry with you for not keeping me more informed as to your doings, your relationships, your dreams, I cannot be at this time of our approaching Holy Days. May you continue to receive God's blessings as you have been since you left this country. I hope you will pass on some of these blessings to us, as we surely can use them. Grandmother Lowenstein mentioned how much you have grown and that you are a proper young lady.

There are so many questions you never answered: What do you want to be when you grow up? Still, a doctor like Wolfgang and me? The dream of keeping you with us in Leipzig and studying medicine is gone forever. I despise the arrangement Wolfgang was forced to make with the German government, but I have resigned myself to it. I will be better off across the ocean than in a concentration camp. I shall continue my medical studies, as soon as I'm able, wherever I am able. My career may be a long time in coming. I hope to achieve it either in USA or in South America, depending on the visa I get. Please write me in detail of your dreams and desires, your friends: what does your foster father do—is he in business like Pappa? The children, do they like you?

I will be working for a lovely family, who has taken me in as their own. The children are delightful, and Rudi—who is your age—is helping me with my English. The laboratory work is not particularly exciting, but it is in the medical field and that is what counts. Please write soon. Enjoy the Holy Days and note my new address.

Your devoted sister—Gerda

That time in my memory …

As much as I have always thought about the romantic circumstances of my sister's marriage, I was totally devastated by her separation from her husband, Wolfgang Gasper. How much more of a shock it must have been for her to be so completely ousted from his life! I don't know what leverage was brought against them; suffice it to say that he was "retrained" as a military physician, and she was eventually able to continue with her medical studies in Brazil.

I understood that my former brother-in-law made some sort of arrangement with the government to let her continue her studies abroad. Still waiting, she was ever hopeful and in the meantime worked in Bremen.

Gerda eventually did become a doctor of psychiatry, married another psychiatrist and had a son, who became a heart surgeon. Her dream of my becoming a doctor never came to realization, but will perhaps be achieved through my granddaughter, a graduate of the U.S. Naval Academy, but now serving as a doctor in the U.S. Air Force.

As I mentioned previously, it was Gerda and Karin who became my intimates in my awkward years. Gerda's strength in the midst of all her problems was my model of inspiration.

Meanwhile, I was going back to school in Winnetka, but still had the feeling I was going to have to change schools since there were persistent rumors of moving to Highland Park across the Cook County line. I hoped and prayed it wasn't so: I had already said so many goodbyes to so many people that I cared about.

September 17, 1935

Dear Little Daughter,

Your letter of the 4th of September just arrived, and, as always, we hold our breath for good news from you. It makes our burdens so much easier. We bear it for the sake of G-d, in whom we trust. We hope for the day when we all can be together, and trust that Uncle Ernest and Elsie will send us affidavits soon.

So for these Holy Days we send you our blessings and prayers, that G-d gives us the strength and patience to carry the heavy burden we must shoulder. We do not pray for "next year in Jerusalem", but in the USA with all our children, and that includes Gerda, who is determined to emigrate. There really is no hope for her and Wolfgang to get together again. As we have mentioned before, they removed him from his post at the Leipzig hospital for "retraining" and eventual assignment as a military health officer. They need all the doctors they can get. What a tragedy.

Our holidays will be quiet, as not as many friends can attend services as before. Some people are afraid to travel, since each station subjects them to scrutiny by uniformed officials. Others are simply getting too old to travel. But Mamma as always is ready with hospitality for whoever comes. Give our best wishes to your foster parents and our gratitude for all they are doing for us.

Your ever-devoted, Pappa

That time in my memory ...

Although not many people came to our little synagogue anymore, there were still enough from the surrounding towns to make more than a "minyan."[2] Mamma had help with hospitality from some of her bolder Christian neighbors who brought fruitcakes, milk, and lemonade.

It was like a miracle to see Mamma blossom as a hostess again. She was an artist when it came to food and could make the most mundane ingredients become a culinary masterpiece, probably taking after her Alsatian mother. She could take a piece of beef, lots of vegetables and a glass of wine, and make a dish fit for a king. I like to think I inherited her gifts as my children still beg me for dishes like "Grandma used to make."

---

2.   Traditionally Jewish services could not be held unless ten men who had been bar mitzvah'd were present. This could present a problem for small Jewish communities under the repressive Nazi regime.

As I had promised, I spent the holidays with my aunt and uncle and their children in Chicago. Although they lived in the hotel where they worked, their apartment was very small. The children had to sleep in a converted storage room with dark green curtains dividing them from the storage, and a bright springy one dividing the boys sleeping space from their sister's. Although the rooms were Spartan, they were furnished with the hotel's good furniture.

Auntie hosted a dinner for all the Lowenstein relatives—I didn't know there were that many in the United States. Admittedly, some who had been born here were Americanized and weren't at all concerned about the families still left in Europe. I couldn't figure out why, between all of them, they couldn't bring my family out, until I realized that the sponsoring family had to have a generous income that could support at least two families—and none of them had that. Although, by European standards they were well off with cars and vacations in Florida, I learned that not everybody's priorities were the same.

September 23, 1935

Dear Little Thea,

Today was really a red-letter day, with two letters from you and mail from all sides, including one from Gerda. As we approach the New Year, we take stock of the many things for which we are still grateful. We still have the house, our dignity, and our faith in G-d. Finally we have a picture of you—but you look so serious, as if the weight of the world were on your shoulders and not on ours. Never mind the teeth braces; you will have a beautiful smile again, I promise you.

Today they buried our loyal old postmaster, who always had us first on the list when your letters came. We always saved him your stamps, and he was so delighted with them. We saw all your old girlfriends at the funeral, and quietly they slipped us the enclosed card to you. It is so sad: even greeting old friends is now forbidden. The men in the leather coats watch everyone. Your letters are about our only contact with the sanity of the outside world, their bright young attitude showing us the hope in another world. So let us pray that in the New Year, we will have our affidavits and start a new life. Even at my age, I am not afraid to begin again. Hard work has ever been our family ethic, all my life; hard work and compassion.

For now, as always, your devoted Pappa

That time in my memory ...

Pappa found ways of being optimistic even in the most trying circumstances. The fact that he could project as far as their fall and winter survival, something many people could not do, is a tribute to his faith. Fall and winter had the highest suicide rates in Europe. Interestingly enough, there were not as many among the Jews as there were in the general German public.

School was going into full swing with our winter program and I finally learned how to diagram a sentence. I felt so isolated, however, in my worries about Europe. No one here, certainly not the children, seemed to comprehend that concern. What was more disconcerting was that very few of the adults seemed to share it either. The newspapers were full of what was happening here with concerns about jobs and the final relief from the depression, which had such a devastating grip on the country. Thanks to FDR and his programs, there was much growth in economic stability of this country. What they wrote about Europe was not so much the economic restriction on

Jews and all of Germany but the anticipation of the 1936 Olympics, and how Germany would be a showcase to the world.

12

October 1935

HEADLINES OF THE DAY:

ADDIS ABABA—Mussolini's Armies Invade Ethiopia; Haile Selassie Vows to Fight Back

ETHIOPIA—Italian Planes Bomb Towns of Adowa and Adigrat; 1700 Die

GENEVA—League of Nations Finds Italy at Fault for War; Moves for Sanctions

WASHINGTON—FDR Orders Arms Embargo on Italy and Ethiopia

BERLIN—German Ministry of Culture Bans "Decadent Jazz" from All German Radio Stations

NEW YORK—Gershwin's "Porgy and Bess" Opens in New York to Critical Audiences

October 21, 1935

Dearest Little Thea,

Now I shall answer your last letter which, to your credit, came in good time. I am glad that all is well again—that you caught up on your sleep, reading, and, above all, writing to the relatives. Please don't misunderstand; we do not expect financial help from your foster parents. I am confident once we have the affidavits and are there, Mamma and I will both be able to find work through relatives and friends. Of course, it won't allow the life we had led up to 1934, but it will be a life of peace, free from fear. That is all we ask. That, and to be together again as a family. As our world gets narrower, and it does, there is really nothing to anticipate but sorrow and depression of the spirit. Even the circle of our relatives grows smaller every day. The ones in Annweiler have been requested to come to the consulate in Stuttgart, and should be underway to USA by year's end. Uncle sold his business and estate in Heusweiler and will be heading for Luxemburg, where cousin Gerda gave birth to a healthy boy two weeks ago.

My loyal customers in the outlying area have been told that their winter relief aid will stop if they spend it in any Jewish establishment. Some of them are paying their debts in farm goods, which is fine for we shall at least have food. Last week, we set Grandfather's headstone. I can't help but think of what fun you used to have together. How he carefully pared you an apple, how he helped you identify wildflowers, how he firmly said, "I won't be alive anymore when she leaves."

How it all came true.

I think he would be happy knowing how it all turned out for you. Mamma will ask you to send any clothing you can to Ruth. We can no longer get a dressmaker to work for us.

Dearest little daughter, please don't think we are dispirited: our hopes are still high, but the urgency is great. I am not Isaiah looking into the future; I am only being realistic when I look at the years ahead as more and more of our people are "resettled" in concentration camps. Meanwhile our joy is in knowing you are safe and enjoying a life we could not give you in Germany anymore.

Your devoted Pappa

That time in my memory ...

The pressure of knowing my responsibilities to everyone was getting to me at that time. Now, I think that it is something that has governed all of my life's actions, and continues to do so. It is something that grew as I got older and made me more competitive in everything I attempted. It also explains this drive for excellence that has dogged me to this day. I finally recognize it.

I often thought of my grandfather and the wonderful lessons he taught me—lessons that are with me still. He suffered horribly from throat cancer and in the last summer of his life, he took me on nature walks that I have never forgotten. In my new life, I always felt more at ease with nature than with people. I had my favorite nook in a tree, a rock on the beach, and a place in the park where violets grew. There was talk of the family moving to a bigger house, but I paid little attention as I felt sure I could continue school until the end of the school year. I was also given a new piano teacher, a young woman, not as romantic about music as the young man who had been teaching me. All the girl students were in love with him; I was no exception and worked twice as hard for his approval. The new teacher was wonderfully knowledgeable and surprisingly passionate about the art she loved. I was proud I was picked to play with her at our student recital. "Für Elise" by Beethoven has been a favorite of mine ever since, and opened up the whole new world of piano compositions.

October 28, 1935

My Dear Little Thea,

Your letter arrived post haste in spite of the terrible weather raging over the Atlantic. We were so glad to hear that the cold you caught at the tennis matches is better and that you are back at school.

So it did come about, as you suspected and you now live in Highland Park. Another change, you must be in a new school and we hope it is as challenging as the one in Winnetka with as many activities. You mention that your piano and dancing lessons are still in Winnetka, so you do see your old friends as well as make new ones. Your other activities—the trips to the Saturday children's concerts in Chicago—continue to provide joyful learning experiences for you and should ease the pain of a move to another school. How many children from your school go to these cultural outings? The new house looks very elegant, as the picture of you and your big dog indicates. I can see why you like to read in your window seat with the bookcases. They look quite well filled. Mamma and I will try to send you as many of your old books as we can find. Naturally, Ruth is reluctant to give up many of them, as they are one of the few pleasures she has.

You must be very cozy by your fireplace. It is one thing we share. The oven in the kitchen with its broad seats offers us warmth and comfort. In this blustery weather, we sit there, listen to music, write, read, play cards, and in general spend our lives waiting for those all-important papers.

You mustn't feel bad about writing us all your good news, when we have so little to report but negative events. Your news is something we live for. Although Ruth cries a lot when she hears how beautiful everything is for you, she stops and is a picture of joy when she gets your packages with all the good things in them.

We must have patience. This, too, will come to an end. As always, our best to your foster family.

Your grateful Pappa

That time in my memory ...

Yes, we moved to another grand estate, this time in Deere Park in Highland Park, Illinois. The house this time was not as cozy as the other one had been. It was like a Georgian manor house in an English country park, complete with porte cochère (formal covered entrance) and winding stone drive. The rooms were larger and grander than our former house, and the first floor had huge French doors overlooking Lake

Michigan. The dining room could easily seat forty people. The library was huge with real books, not just false fronted as so many were. The kitchen was all stainless steel and very impressive, but with Mrs. Darnell in charge, it still became an oasis of warmth and comfort.

Mine was one of a suite of rooms which I shared with the children and Nanny. It had a fireplace and window seats with bookcases which instantly became my favorite reading place. Captain, our big Great Dane, became my faithful companion. As I mentioned before, the other children were afraid because he was so large and as playful as he was, he would invariably knock them down with his huge paws. But he was my protector and slept in my room next to the fire.

The new school was another excellent, advanced-in-study school called Braeside. I was disappointed that I had to leave my friends in Winnetka School, but I could still see them at Fortnightly and on our Saturday music outings with Dr. Stock in Chicago. Braeside School was just inside the Lake County line, a separation from Cook County which encompasses Chicago and the North Shore as far as Glencoe. The school, although it was public, ran much more along the lines of a more informal private school. Classes were fairly small, the largest being eighth grade which was my class. We had only one teacher, rather than several for every subject. That meant that he, in this case a Mr. Van Meter, taught not only the academic subjects but art, music, shop, and athletics. Once the children got over their initial curiosity about my accent, they were friendly and accepting. The big hit of course, was Captain, who would accompany me to school. My Saturdays in Chicago, with Dr. Stock, were still the highlight of the week. Dr. Stock had a worse German accent than mine, so that made me feel better. I only later realized how his great influence on my love for classical music was to become.

13

November 1935

HEADLINES OF THE DAY:

GERMANY—Hitler Promises to Remove Anti-Jewish Signs during 1936 Olympics

GERMANY—Reich Announces German Jewish Athletes Will Be Restricted from Olympics Participation

UNITED STATES—U.S. Protestants Ask for Olympic Boycott

PRAGUE—Czechs Arrest 28 Alleged German Spies

CHINA—Japanese Troops Invade Shanghai

ETHIOPIA—2,000 Killed in Italian Air Raid

BERLIN—Reich Declares All Men between 18 to 45 Army Reservists

BERLIN—Reich Makes Non-Belief in Nazism Grounds for Divorce

November 5, 1935

Dear Little Thea,

Your letter arrived in record time and finally we figured out a schedule: if we write Tuesday or Wednesday and the letters reach the boat by Thursday, they should reach you in a week; unless we're lucky enough to have them on a quick liner like the 'Bremen'. Some day, God willing, there will be instant communications. At any rate, please keep them coming as steadily as you have been doing. Don't feel guilty about writing of all the wonderful people you meet, things that are happening to you at school and play, your beautiful home: all that touches your life—all of which makes for an exciting future for you; one that will benefit all of us.

Sunday it will be a year since I took you to Hamburg and I pray that Mamma, Ruth and I can take that trip again soon. Please write the relatives here when you can. They too live on hope and G-d's good graces. We still feel luckier than most.

Until our next "letter meeting", be blessed and enjoy your beautiful life.

Your devoted Pappa

That time in my memory ...

There is little to add but that the guilt feelings of having things so beautiful grew stronger and, strangely, I grew homesick. I can only explain it today by saying that, in some way, I felt that I should have shared the hard times with them. It was hard to believe that a year had passed since Pappa took me to the ship in Hamburg. So much had already happened: I couldn't imagine what was yet to come. I would often ask myself, "Why me?" Why did my life have so many positives? Why was I being rewarded with so many blessings? At the moment school work overshadowed everything. For the first time I was overwhelmed by the amount of subjects and was having some difficulty meeting what I considered my best. I dropped voice lessons, but with the hope that someday I could resume them.

The family talked about our winter vacation, but I was happiest to sit by my fire with my books, and my dog, especially as winter was closing in. I also got into the habit of reading to Betty Ann and Larry. Tagne was delighted when I took over that share of her duties. The dramatics of the reading delighted the children, and soon I was reading to the entire family after dinner. We even wrote plays around our nightly pastime and these were performed to a most enthusiastic audience of Aunt Anne, Uncle Harry and any of the servants who were around and cared to watch it.

For Halloween we had a huge party at the farm. It also gave me a chance to ride Rolli again. I hadn't seen him all summer. All the Perlsteins and Agazims were there with popcorn, cider, Brunswick stew and pumpkin pie. There was a man strumming a banjo and everybody sang "Jimmy Crack Corn" and other old-time American songs. Norman Rockwell would have been proud of this American scene. It seemed so natural to be part of it. Europe and its shadowy future seemed far away, I couldn't imagine ever being part of it at times like this.

Letter from Gerda

November 6, 1935

My dearest Thea,

As you can see I am trying, but you can also see how little [English] I remember. However, I will make every effort to learn along with you. Please write your replies in English. It will be a help to both of us.

So my dear little sister, it's over a year since you left. Can you still remember? As I learned from our parents in their last letter, you are having a wonderful life with your adopted family, that school is very interesting for you, and that you are losing your German accent, with all kinds of lessons. You know the English writer, George Bernard Shaw, wrote a delightful story about an English girl named Eliza Doolittle, who was taught proper English by a Professor Higgins. It was Mr. Shaw's interpretation of "Pygmalion and Galatea." Thea can become Galatea and learn proper English. Be like a sponge. Absorb everything and you will learn things you never dreamed of.

I wish I could see you. You don't know how I live through your adventures. With the divorce now final, I am still in shock, but I have a good job and wonderful people around me. I hope I can either go to the States or there is a chance for South America, but with my bad luck—but you are too young to understand that. Just remember how happy we all were together and that Wolfgang loved all of us. Your foster mother sounds like a wonderful lady. Please give her my gratitude for being so wonderful to my little sister. I know you'll not disappoint them.

As of the 1st of January, 1936, I will have another address. I will be working for a different doctor. It looks very promising to be back in my profession and continue my studies. Not that I haven't enjoyed being the companion of these two lovely children. They too are learning English, so we have English tea parties.

So my dearest little sister, be of good cheer. Write often so I can also enjoy your life. You have such a great future ahead.

Your loving sister, Gerda

That time in my memory ...

Through this letter, my sister became an even greater heroine than before. Her courage in facing life, in her circumstances, inspired me even further, to achieve. The story of Pygmalion was always an amusing remembrance and I literally went through the marble-in-the-mouth experience to get rid of my rolling "Rs", and to modulate my voice.

Gerda's English writing was very quaint. We eventually reverted to German again with English words interspersed. Strangely enough, as I write to her now in Brazil, where she lives retired in a convent, it is in English.

Being in touch with Gerda added a touch of romance to my life. I dreamt of her coming to the United States and marrying one of those nice dashing young men who were on the periphery of my life with the Perlsteins. According to Aunt Anne, they were much too old for me, but not Gerda. I kept arguing with her, "Some day that won't make so much difference. Look at Peaches Browning and her Sugar Daddy." This at the moment was the big May-December romance in the tabloids. She only laughed and asked how I could expect an older man to keep up with all that I had planned to do in my life.

Of course, she was right. Marrying Army Lt. Harry Lindauer in 1946 enriched my life with worldwide travel, continued studies of the arts, and networking with fascinating people all over the world.

November 18, 1935

Dear Little Thea,

Today our roles are reversed, and Mamma will write the bulk of the letter, as I returned from quite a circuit; a roundtrip to family and friends who needed their travel tickets and insurance for their emigration. So it seems strange that with little business in the store, I should be so busy filling out travel tickets and insurance papers. I came home to find both Mamma and Ruth studying their English lessons and that is good. I think you should write some of your letter in English, as it will be a big help to us.

Ruth is very excited about the prospect of a big package of clothes. It will be Chanukah and Christmas all in one, with the prospect of a new picture, a studio portrait—whatever that is. Mamma is very excited, as we shall have a trip to Frankfurt to hear Richard Tauber before he leaves for England. When someone as great and well known as he must leave the country, Mamma doesn't feel so bad. Then, too, she has found a dressmaker who will come in the evening, and so she is very pleased to be getting a new wardrobe. She is already planning a wardrobe to take to the states and is optimistic for the first time in months.

And so life goes on, up and down. Children are born and the aged die. Sometimes it is reversed, as several children died of influenza and tuberculosis. That is something Mr. Hitler cannot master. Perhaps being isolated makes us less vulnerable to disease. I feel G-d is still on our side.

I am very tired so receive my love and kisses—Ruth wants to write yet before her 8:30 curfew.

Your loving Pappa

That time in my memory ...

Richard Tauber[1] was the Number One tenor of both operatic and musical stage in Germany. Mamma adored his voice. I suppose today she would be called a "Richard Tauber Groupie." That he had to emigrate surprised no one, as so many fine artists had to go into exile. Whenever he was in the area, Mamma would give a theater party. As I think of it now, I clipped out articles about famous people who went into exile and cut short brilliant careers in Europe. Some survived and went onto greater

---

1.   Richard Tauber (1891-1948) was Germany's best-known singer of operettas and one of the first real matinee idols of the post-WWI period in Central Europe. He emigrated to Great Britain, where he died.

fame, but some did not. I'm thinking particularly of another wonderful singer we knew, Joseph Schmidt[2], a wonderful tenor who ended up in obscurity in Switzerland and never made it to the Met, because he was supposedly "too short."

Although he went on to write musical scores for Errol Flynn movies, Erich Korngold[3] was never appreciated for his magnificent classic masterpieces. Many years later, after his Hollywood success, he would laughingly point out that his life was really saved by Robin Hood. This was the film for which Warner Brothers brought him to Hollywood just in time to escape the Austrian Anschluss (annexation) and the dire consequences for so many people. Others who duplicated their European successes were Max Reinhardt[4] and Franz Werfel[5], who made their refugee status most acceptable. That was the classification I hoped to reach. At times, I can still hear echoes of the "poor refugees" in dark whispers by the so-called privileged society of which I was rapidly becoming one. It seems absurd in my circumstances to be classified as a "poor refugee."

2.   Josef Schmidt (1904-1942) was a Rumanian-born tenor with a distinctive, beautiful voice. Only 5 feet tall, he appeared more on radio and in recital, although his 1933 movie, "A Song goes Around the World" is a classic. Schmidt's death was particularly tragic: Forced to cross illegally into Switzerland after the Nazi takeover of Vichy France, he died of a heart attack as an internee in a detention camp.

3.   Erich Wolfgang Korngold (1897-1957) was a child prodigy and classical composer who became famous for his movie scores, including "Captain Blood", "The Adventures of Robin Hood", and "The Sea Hawk."

4.   Max Reinhardt (1873-1943) was a renowned Austrian stage director and impresario. He came to Hollywood to direct a Warner Bros. movie in 1935 and remained in the United States until his death.

5.   Franz Werfel (1890-1945) was Austrian-born and a famous novelist, poet, and playwright. He is best known for his novel "The Song of Bernadette" which was made into a widely-beloved movie about the Catholic saint.

14

December 1935

GERMANY—Jewish Doctors Forced to Resign from Practice in All Private Hospitals

CHINA—Chiang Kai-Shek Named Chinese President

UNITED STATES—Cold Spell in U.S. Kills 212 People; Government Pledges Relief for Victims' Families

UNITED STATES—Sinclair Lewis Warns of Dangers of Fascism in "It Can't Happen Here"

FRANCE—Nobel Prize for Chemistry Awarded to Irene and Frederic Joliot-Curie; She Becomes First Second-Generation Nobel Winner

Letter from Gerda:

December 2, 1935

Dear Little Thea,

I'm at home keeping Mamma company. Pappa is still on his travels and thanks to G-d is still alright. We are always in a state of anxiety. That is why your letters are so important; but this week we waited in vain. Perhaps it's the terrible winter storms that are the cause, but please keep up your weekly communication. It is so important to know what you are doing and learning. With the ice and snow, the children are ice-skating. As much as I love it, I don't have the same enjoyment as I used to have—I go to please Ruth, who is so little in the company of other children. Most of the time, we sit in this warm and pleasant room, do needlework, read, and listen to Mamma's beloved opera arias on the phonograph. On the radio is nothing but propaganda and marching songs.

Your classmates, though they cannot openly acknowledge it, are still interested in you and so are your former teachers. Please write them as you are learning things they can only dream about. You say you are in 8th grade and will graduate into high school next year. Please give us some more details about your school work, your piano and dancing lessons, and your weekly trip to a symphony appreciation class in Chicago. I have heard of Dr. Stock, he is a very fine conductor. Ruth and I play a game in which we try to picture all your activities and the people with whom you enjoy them all. Are you obedient and caring to your foster parents? It is so important as it is sure to bring them joy and thanks for their goodness to you. Gratitude is the most important element in everything you do. I'm sure with your new knowledge of English you can communicate much better with them especially the little ones. Ruth thinks it's funny that you have lessons with marbles in your mouth to get rid of your strong German accent.

I spoke before of an English play by George Bernard Shaw, "Pygmalion" in which a professor tries to teach the heroine proper English. It is a very good play. Perhaps you will read it in high school. Thea, my dear, you speak very highly of your foster parents, your beautiful home and all the fantastic things you are doing. All that costs a lot of money. You never speak of what your foster father does to have all that money. You say he is an important man. I am assuming that he is a doctor, lawyer, has a factory, or is in politics, for it takes that type of position to live that way. Please so not misunderstand, we are not trying to sound greedy, only curious. The organization only wrote to our parents that they are well-to-do people who opened their home and hearts to you.

Elsie and Aunt Lydia write they are very rich, and you are overly protected from a lot of people, that you cannot go anywhere even to the relatives without the protection of their chauffeur. When they all went to have tea with you—they felt honored and impressed, but not comfortable. I was sorry to hear that. They are good people and also wish you happiness. Sometimes it is a stress on Mamma that you don't communicate with them more often. Forgive me for writing so bluntly. As a future psychiatrist, I have all these questions and anxiety causing element that can make your future bright and happy or become obstacles to your well being.

But enough lecturing for today. Continue your bright happy life. Pretty soon we will be writing 1936. We hope it will be a better year, since it will bring the Olympic Games to Berlin and make a showcase out of Germany. We think the Nazis will tone everything down a bit. They have even erected signs "Kraft durch Freude" (strength through joy) at the temporary collecting stations they have created.

Dear little Thea, pretty soon I won't be able to address you that way anymore. You are growing into a real young lady. When you speak of your dancing school with boys and girls together, it sounds so unreal from what our boys and girls are taught. We are so grateful you can grow up in that healthy atmosphere. Pappa will be back to write you next week, but now for all of us, with love,

Your big sister, Gerda

That time in my memory ...

There still was a curiosity about my foster parents that made me uncomfortable. It also caused some tension between me and the Chicago relatives. My foster parents invited them to family celebrations, but since they feel they could not reciprocate, they declined many of them. I did visit in Chicago when it is possible, particularly on holidays.

Gerda, as always, was more clinically curious than the rest of the family, but I still did not feel like discussing all my feelings, even with her. How can I share trivialities about the success of a party or enough flowers for a table setting with my dear ones, whose very existence was being threatened? One of my friends, called me "a party pooper", because I chastised her about one of those trivialities. After that I kept my mouth shut and my eyes and ears open.

I liked Braeside School. The children were more modest and sharing than some of my classmates in Winnetka. Still, I was reluctant to ask some home, as there never was that relaxed atmosphere I felt in their houses.

But life was full. I continued with lessons and particularly on the piano since we had a grand piano that was also a player piano, performing classical music. I would give wonderful "concerts" for the family sounding, of course, like Paderewski and Horowitz.

The family talks were about winter vacation in Florida and swimming in the ocean. I was still Europe-oriented, and not too impressed spending the Christmas holidays away from the traditional one with ice and snow. Other than the young children and middle aged parents, I met very few young people my age in these vacation spots. But it seemed like one more adventure I hadn't tried.

December 3, 1935

Dear Little Daughter,

We were so happy to receive your letter from November 10th, but I decided to wait with our answer until Gerda arrived. She has found a wonderful job with a doctor who knows Wolfgang and is delighted to have her work with him. Then she can also continue her psychiatric studies. Mamma is so glad to have her company, and so is Ruth, who still has trouble going to sleep in the nursery. We are thinking of moving her to the 2nd floor so she is closer to us.

The affidavits from Uncle Ernst fell through. I won't go into detail, but suffice it to say that we must turn elsewhere for these all-important papers. Perhaps when the Annweiler relatives are there, or perhaps through a man with whom I had business over the years we can get papers. But for the time being we must shelve that dream until we gather new strength and resources. I hate to see Mamma so disappointed.

You sound very excited about your trip to Florida, and your ability to go swimming there in the wintertime. It is as good as going to California, only not as far away. Your school pageant sounds very colorful. I hope you send a program since you won a prize painting it. I still cannot picture you in anything but the medical profession, but I know that whatever you do, you will do well.

We envy you the Florida trip, as the weather here is dreadful; heavy rain storms with sleet and icy streets. But since we are not out much, it doesn't bother us. We only see a few loyal neighbors, the Heilmanns among them. Both his son and nephew have been questioned by the Gestapo about their "antigovernment" activities. All that means is that they do not follow the accepted party line, and are not afraid to speak out. I do not want to write about politics, as they exist here. As a 13-year-old, you cannot be that interested, and as a man in his 50's, I should know how to stay out of trouble.

Have a wonderful time in the sunshine with your foster family. I pray for them and thank G-d for their goodness. We can never repay them.

Your devoted Pappa

That time in my memory …

The heavily censored newspapers in Germany were expected to rigidly toe the party line. The family-owned paper of the Heilmanns was considered too independent in its ideas and had brought down official Ministry of Information censure, particularly on the younger members of the family. I didn't quite understand about the Heilmanns' antigovernment activities and that the young men needed to be "re-educated" along party lines. At that time, the subtleties of political re-education was something I could not quite comprehend. I know that children were taught the new history and of course, the adult population turned to the myths of the Third Reich. How they could re-educate adults under coercion was not comprehensible to me—you either believed in something, or you did not.

Once again, Uncle Ernest's affidavit declaration was not financially great enough to vouch for the family's income, should they come to the States. The fear of "going on welfare" was always a question in the recession-riddled government agenda. Father's age and physical condition, regarding his cataracts, may also have been a questionable factor. Needless to say, we were all very disappointed, and I couldn't understand why Pappa wouldn't let me ask the Perlsteins to help. But that was his decision. He still hoped to get the necessary affidavits from all the relatives and some former business associates.

However, it all took away much of the anticipation of the Florida trip. On the other hand, our school pageant for the parents was a success in as much as it gave every child a chance to contribute. Since I won the program cover painting contest, I was very proud and a career in art became my main interest. I started a drawing diary of daily events and I wish I still had these mementos now no longer in my keeping.

December 12, 1935

Dear Little Daughter,

I am finally back from my long trip of helping other people leave, wishing we were that far. It is not as easy as it was when you left. The circumstances were so different. I thank G-d for the foresight he gave me. We're going into 1936—but there is very little joy in the Christmas season. Chanukah will be very sparse this year, but Mamma managed to get two geese for the holidays, and Ruth got a new coat from the Herzes, and the dresses you sent are beautiful. She is so proud of her new wardrobe. Do not send a Shirley Temple doll, even though you have outgrown playing with dolls, and Ruth has not. Rather, keep it as an incentive for hope. That way our time to leave may seem closer at hand. The trip made me realize how long and complicated the wait can be.

Germany is sprucing up for the Olympic Games. They want the world to see what a showcase they have become. I think we can expect some relaxation of the harsh persecution, but it is unrealistic to expect that it will be consequential and permanent. This is according to those who still look out for my interest. Some day their story, too, will be told. Remember, there are some good Germans as well as bad ones. Please don't forget that. You speak of the family going to Florida, where it is warm. Here everything is ice and snow. It is even too cold for Ruth to go skating. It was a blessing to have Gerda here to keep Mamma and Ruth company during my absence.

I will not try to write you in Florida, as you will be gone only for two weeks. Rather, we will greet the New Year together. Mamma is making *Glühwein (Spiced wine)* for *Sylvester [New Years Eve]* in 1935 to welcome the New Year of 1936. May we celebrate 1937 together as a family again!

As always—Your devoted Pappa

That time in my memory ...

Pappa was right in his assessment: Germany tried to tone down the Anti-Semitism, and spruce up its cities and towns. Even concentration camps bore signs, "Kraft durch Freude" (Strength through Joy), and were given flower-bedecked entrances. The inmates of the so-called labor camps were formed into orchestras and sports teams for the" entertainment" of the visitors. Even the U.S newspapers picked up the positive reports, but it was all only on the surface. Although the Nazis would reluctantly allow some American Jews to compete in the Olympics, all the German Jews and their sports clubs were banned from participating. Many years later, I found out that my husband who was a champion runner was not allowed to compete. This was one more reason why he emigrated to the United States.

One blessing that came out of the camp orchestras, the musicians that were good enough to play for officials were sent to Theresienstadt, the model camp, where they survived the war, and were able to return home afterwards.

One such man was Isaac Hamburger whom we visited long after the war in Seligenstadt, Germany, southeast of Frankfurt. At the age of 84, he gave us a beautiful recital of Brahms and Schubert one sunny afternoon. Music had saved his life and that of his brother, since they had both provided entertainment for officials of the Nazi party.

Meanwhile I spent Christmas vacation with the family in Florida. I would rather have been with my campmates at the Chicago reunion, but didn't think of it in time to register. The house we had on the beach was to me too ostentatious to be a beach house—it had a terrazzo enclosed fountain in a centrally located round hall looking out at the ocean. It felt like too much gilt on the lily, but then so many of the houses there were in the same style—not nature-related as they are today. One plus, I could do my required school reading assignment sitting in the sun. On my return, I had to report on five books. It seemed so strange to be sitting on a beach, while the family was struggling through ice and snow. Florida seemed like a never, never land with no real concern for the outside world—even for the rest of the United States, for that matter.

December 21, 1935

My dear Child,

My birthday [December 16th] came and went. Mamma, Gerda, and Ruth gave me a little party. For a moment, we all wished you were here, but we also know how much better it is for you over there. Gerda bought a new Beethoven recording in honor of our mutual birthday, the 16th of December. At least he is still allowed to be played in Germany.

We thought of you in the sunshine of Florida while we have all that ice and snow. Many children are sick. School closed earlier than usual for the Christmas holidays. We did some Christmas business, mainly the French goods that Uncle Herman left when he closed his stores. The people are hungry for foreign goods, but dare not show it. Everything that is not German is decadent.

Soon we will write 1936. What will it bring? We hope like the children of Israel in the Exodus—a release from this nightmare. We are still lucky and have more to be hopeful about than many others. I am still able to provide for Mamma and Ruth. We have a barter system with some of my customers just as they had in early America. They bring me the bounty of the farms for the things I am able to provide for them. I have been fortunate; no one has denounced me for still calling them by their first name. In some areas, the Jewish traders have been cited for calling their old customers and friends by their first names. I received a birthday card signed by many, many people: George, Peter, Heinrich, etc.

By now you must be having a wonderful holiday in the sun. Do you celebrate New Year's as we do here, with thick soup and herring salad? Probably not, but something gay and memorable to see out the old and welcome the new. As ever, with all good wishes to the Perlstein family.

Your devoted Pappa

P.S. Soon, I hope to write them my gratitude in proper English. I have been practicing with Gerda.

That time in my memory ...

Pappa brought much of Uncle Herman's merchandise to the store. Since it was French, it mysteriously—and unofficially—sold immediately, with no interference from official parties.

I enjoyed Boca Raton, Florida, where the family had rented a big beach house for all the relatives, distant and close. Again, as I had mentioned before, it was so unreal and removed from Daddy and the family as they underwent greater and greater restrictions at the hands of the Nazis.

New Years Eve is a happy, hopeful event no matter where you are. For us on the beach it was a fire on the sand, with good food and company, and anticipation of the year ahead. I was able to speak to my campmates at the Chicago reunion, and that made me feel better.

It was interesting to observe the different people that were attracted to Florida. Many live there in retirement, but some come only to escape the northern winters. Some have their own houses, but many rent apartments in expensive hotels. There seemed to be no lack of money, and the Depression seemed far away and seemed to have missed Florida entirely. That too was an illusion, as I learned later. The difference was that the drifting, jobless, didn't have to shiver in the mild Florida temperatures. Those who developed Florida, the Flaglers, the Dukes, must have had some astute insights into what was to be the future of the United States under an economic system that provided so many opportunities to so many.

15

January 1936

HEADLINES OF THE DAY:

BERLIN—German Officials Say Nazi Treatment of Jews is Not League of Nations Business

LONDON—Denied Parity with Western Nations, Japan Quits Naval Talks

CHICAGO—Joe Louis KO's Charley Tetzlaff in First Round

PARIS—Premier Pierre Laval Resigns over Diplomatic Failure to Solve Ethiopian Crisis

LONDON—King George V Dies; Edward VIII Succeeds to English Throne

January 6, 1936

My dearest little Daughter,

You are back from your holiday in Florida, burnt brown and freckled, I'm sure, and eager to start your schooling again. It is interesting that your teacher wants you to do a project on your life in Germany. I cannot imagine your saying anything about the misery of today, as you were so fortunate not to live through it. You never felt anti-Semitism as it exists now ... I'm willing to wager there are places in the United States where it exists, but not openly, certainly not practiced by the government.

Your foster father's friends, the governor of Illinois, Senator Lehman, Justice Frankfurter, who sits on the Supreme Court, Bernard Baruch, the President's advisor, the many professors and people who create your culture—all were able to achieve their goals in spite of their religious beliefs. Know, my dear child, that you live in a country where everyone is free to achieve. Never mind that you cannot join a church sorority. The restrictions are their privilege. On the other hand, you were in a beautiful summer camp and had a great birthday celebrated in a Jewish club. They, too, are selective; that is the way of life. Until Hitler came, there were more marriages like Liselotte and Oscar, Gerda and Wolfgang—we became one family, and no one thought of Christian and Jew. You must not let what is happening here today distort your feeling about the individual people. Love and respect are the strongest virtues we can express.

But enough lectures for today. Work hard at your grades.

You have that wonderful "book-nook" for studying and reading. There are so many wonderful books that you can explore, I wish I could explore them with you, especially the books by Mr. Dickens and Mr. Shaw.

For today, as always—Your devoted Pappa.

That time, in my memory ...

Whatever horrors the Nazis perpetrated, they cannot equal the devastation of splitting loving families who had followed different faiths for generations. It is a tragedy that I cannot forgive. It still haunts me. Even today, I face intermarriage with trepidation, although my own family is still very much involved with it. Our family contains both Catholic and Protestant members who live in harmony and mutual respect, those key factors in relationships.

I had read my assignment of books during my Florida holiday and fell in love with the "Anne of Green Gables" series. It was a bit of America I knew little about. So, too, were the Mark Twain stories. They made life so wonderfully simple. Charles Dickens overwhelmed me with his richness of language; Shaw with his witty cynicism, not yet quite understood.

Although I knew that certain adult books were censored and officially banned in the United States, I could not imagine book burning as it was taking place in Germany. I believe in the tradition of burying books as the prayer books of old, as a sign of respect and deference for the wisdom they represent. To this day, I keep a copy of Pappa's and Grandfather's Machzer (prayer book), along with the prayer book presented to Mamma on her wedding day by the Baroness Rothschild, on one of my shelves.

Comparative religions and its books have always fascinated me, and the similarity in so many religious philosophies has left me with respect, admiration, and reflection.

January 28, 1936

Dearest Little Thea,

This has been a very severe month as far as the weather is concerned. The snow and ice continue, but we are snug in our house. School has not yet opened for Ruth, as there is still too much illness among the children. She is studying faithfully at home. Although we have not heard anything about our latest request to emigrate, we're all reading our weekly English lessons. It is slow, because we have only ourselves to teach each other.

Ruth looks forward to the "Valentine Present" you promised to send her. It is a holiday we do not know here, but sounds like great fun as many holidays do. We, of course, have *Fastnacht (Shrove Tuesday, Mardi Gras)*, the day before Lent, with all its craziness. Of course, I no longer give my "Buttenreden" (A humorous spoof on politics) of all that goes on around us, but then—neither does anyone else. As I have written previously, you cannot criticize the government, even in jest anymore. There is no humor left to us but an underground publication called "Black Humor", jokes about government officials. These jokes are enough to earn you a prison sentence if you are caught with the book. How foolish, how desperately afraid people are.

How is your project on Germany coming? I wish I could send you other than the propaganda material, but everything else is forbidden or nonexistent. Books, paintings, and music—everything that doesn't represent Germany as blonde, blue-eyed, smiling, and heroic—is declared to be decadent or degenerate. I must not bother you so much with my serious thoughts, but you are growing up and you must know that life contains both joy and pain, optimism and disappointment. When you balance them in acceptance, you can go on living.

Mamma and Ruth send their love and so do I.

Your Pappa

That time in my memory ...

As always, Pappa's philosophy made a deep impression and lifted my spirits, and so did his sense of humor. His critical talks at Mardi Gras time were one way of expressing it.

At times, I felt a deep split in my emotions as to where I was heading and the alternate joy and puzzlement it gave me. My concern about those I left behind made my resolve to succeed even stronger. That grown people were afraid was ever more puzzling.

My project on Germany, with my personal memories as a child growing up there, didn't ring quite true in the light of all that was happening over there. I tried to concentrate on the children who were waiting to get out, even though they came out only in driblets and not in the thousands as had been hoped. For the most part, people didn't feel the anxieties about Germany that I felt: How could they, when they saw pictures of apple-cheeked, smiling children raising their hands in the Nazi salute? It all seemed so normal and right with the world, as if the underlying traditions were impossible to visualize—from their vantage point, safe, across a wide ocean.

16

February 1936

LONDON—Foreign Secretary Anthony Eden says Britain Must be Strong to Prevent War in Europe

INDIA—Jawaharlal Nehru Elected President of Indian National Congress

LONDON—Charlie Chaplin Film "Modern Times" Opens to Huge Audience Success

BERLIN—Germany Arrests 150 Catholic Leaders for Defying Nazi Doctrine

GERMANY—Hitler Opens Winter Olympics at Garmisch-Partenkirchen

WASHINGTON—FDR Signs Second Neutrality Act, Bans Loans to Belligerents

---

February 15, 1936

Dearest Little Daughter,

We received the package of Valentine gifts and were delighted with them. Chocolate, which is forbidden to us under the new law, was a special treat, and so were the cigars. I shall smoke them very sparingly; that way they last longer into the year. I don't know how much longer you can send packages and uncensored letters. So far, our good postmaster has sent everything on to us, but then he is very special, as the old one was.

The weather is clearing; at least now and then we can catch a glimpse of sun and a patch of blue sky. Believe it or not, the almond trees are in bloom. People are beginning to come out of their houses and go about their business. I've turned most of my merchandise over to the other merchants in town. They are sympathetic, and have made me quite a fair offer for anything I have to give them.

There is now a new government movement to exchange Jews for English goods, and to train and resettle the Jews in Palestine. This is fine for the young people, but what of the older generation? Thank goodness for the agencies; they do give us an income.

You have been very quiet about your activities in your last letters. I know you do not ride in the winter, but what about your dancing, writing, and painting? That is indoors so you must still be doing it. You speak of having colds; we hope it is nothing more serious than that. Sometimes when you're growing too fast you also become susceptible to young peoples' diseases. Please let us know, as we are always concerned about you.

Mamma and Ruth have yet to write, specifically their thanks for all the gifts, so I will close. They are busy knitting more warm sweaters; winter is not over yet, despite the blossoming almond trees.

With much affection—Your devoted Pappa

That time in my memory ...

Returning from Florida, I became very aware of the carefree life I was leading and the trials the family was experiencing. It left me very depressed. There was a let down in my activities; and minor plagues, like colds and aching joints, were constantly with me. When I think about it today, those feelings still overwhelm me at times. The Valentine gifts were, again, a joyous break in their bleak lives, and the forbidden chocolates were a real treat.

Can anyone here imagine being forbidden to eat chocolates, look at pictures, read a book or listen to music? To me it was incomprehensible. Here of course I was receiving gifts of growing-up books and items like stationery and records—all the requirements that my education needed and the indulgences of caring people.

My schoolwork, strangely enough, suffered very little from my bleak thoughts, and I still had a lot of what Aunt Anne called "growing pains." She spent a lot of time and effort trying to change my attention to positive activities. Mr. Van Meter, my teacher, was most helpful in my school project on growing up in Germany; I hoped to present it at my graduation.

17

March 1936

HEADLINES OF THE DAY:

GERMANY—Hitler Sends Troops into Rhineland, Defying Locarno & Versailles Treaties

UNITED STATES—FDR Opens Norris Dam in Tennessee; TVA Brings Electric Power to Rural Areas

BERLIN—German Press Warns that Jews Who Vote will be Arrested

MUNICH—Hitler Tells Crowd of 300,000, "Germany's Only Judge is God and Itself"

MADRID—Army Threatens to act if President Azana Cannot Curb Civil Strife

UNITED STATES—Floods Sweep 12 Midwest States; 134 Dead, 200,000 Homeless

March 1, 1936

Dearest Little Daughter,

We did not hear from you this week, but I am sure a letter is on the way. You have been very good about keeping us abreast about what is going on in your life. You know we live for news of you.

Much is changing in the house, since we must move to the second floor. The store will be rebuilt into an apartment, and our living quarters will have a new tenant—someone in the Nazi hierarchy no doubt—to keep an eye on me. Nevertheless, I am pleased we shall have what was the Synagogue rebuilt into our quarters. Grandfather's room and the old bath-chamber will also be part of it, so we shall be comfortable. However, we shall miss the old, cozy kitchen-living room.

With new laws every day, it is difficult to keep up with all of them. Naturally, they all deal with the degradation of the Jews and what they have achieved. Of course, the young people are enthusiastic, and the old are silent and wary. All is for the glory of the Fatherland.

And now, about you. Your new home sounds very grand with your own room with lots of space for books and hobbies. I know you have it filled already. Your friend, the big dog, Captain, sounds almost as big as your horse. I'm sure he takes good care of you, even walking you to school and picking you up. Speaking of school how is your project on Germany coming? I'm sure no one can believe what is going on today, with pictures of smiling children and pretty villages drawing in the tourists.

On the advice of my friends, who are in the know about these matters, I shall be going on another trip, so until I return our love to you.

As always, your loving Pappa

Recollections and Remembrances:

Here again, Pappa was upset about all the changes in the house and their mode of living. It had stood for so many years as a symbol of the strength of our family. I was comforted by the fact that they had Grandfather's rooms, the synagogue, and the grand bathroom. I considered them the essential parts of our home anyway. The interesting thing about houses, like food, they can set a climate of comfort and well-being. In retrospect, although my life pointed to the positive, the difference between that and what my family was experiencing in Germany, left me with a constant feeling of guilt.

Mamma had an odd request at this time: if I could send her some black poplin so that the sisters of Marie's order could make new habits. Marie, our former nursemaid, had joined an order of Ursuline nuns and was now Sister Brigitte. After my sister and I were past her care, "she didn't want any more children", she said and so joined the order. It seemed the fabric was one item that the efficient German Government could not accommodate—it was not in the Thousand Year Reich plans. I had Aunt Anne contact the Catholic Churches in Chicago for help in getting the material for them which they did with efficient briskness. Getting it to Sister Brigitte was another matter: That was handled through the church.

Pappa's out-of-town trips usually meant that the Nazis were planning another propaganda drive against Jewish businesses, and his friends wanted him out of harm's way. Again, their loyalties were a great comfort to him.

School was a very comforting challenge at that point, with graduation not far off. I would be starting high school. It was still a question of where. If we continued living in Highland Park, it would be the high school in that town—if we moved again back to Cook County, it would be New Trier in Winnetka. I could hardly wait to begin this new phase of my life.

March 11, 1936

Dear Little Thea,

I've returned from a very tiring trip to find your letter waiting, and it made me feel much better. I will answer your worried questions, but first must assure you that everything is and will continue to be all right with us. Although I am writing exit cards and ship passage for other people, I cannot write ours until we have an appointment at the consulate and are okayed for emigration. It is not as easy as it once was. As soon as it happens, I promise to notify you. Again, do not approach your foster parents at this time; they have done so much for us already. Let us see how much Uncle Ernest and Uncle Samuel in St. Louis can do for us.

Meanwhile, the house is undergoing many changes. They moved two more families in. Mamma has sold most of the heavy old furniture, as it is too big to fit into the new apartment. We are really sad to see the beautiful pieces go; she took such loving care of them. I remember in particular you sitting in front of the china cabinet and watching your reflection in the cut glass doors. You used to count the china pieces that you could see through them and remember the occasions when they were used, particularly the ones with forget-me-nots which were always your favorites. Ruth, of course, is delighted, since she now has her bed in our room. There are so many memories: The fact that they are pleasant makes it most comforting.

The winter Olympics opened and drew 500,000 spectators from all over the world. The Norwegians are dominating them, and a young girl named Sonja Henje has everyone captivated. She has swept the gold medals for all the figure skating events. She is young and pretty, certainly the image of the Aryan ideal that Mr. Hitler adores.

Now to all that is happening on your side of the ocean: You say you had a fire at your school. Was everyone alright? Are you at another school? Please write more about it.

Your *Fastnacht* (Mardi Gras celebration) sounded wonderful. Did you have pancakes as we do here, and were dressed up in masks and costumes? Ruth still has your little Spanish senorita costume, but is outgrowing it rapidly. You must have taken the little fan with you, because we couldn't find it and had to make one out of gold paper and black lace.

We shall try to get the "Little Women" book in German for Ruth, but foreign books are almost impossible to find. All that is not German or Teutonic is decadent, as I have said before. I must close, as I have many letters to write.

With love from all of us—Your dearest Pappa

P.S. For the first time, your letter had been opened, no doubt looking for illegal money. It was clumsily resealed. I am not too concerned, as your innocence speaks for itself. In the future, I too will watch what I am writing.

—Pappa

The time in my memory ...

The reminder not to ask the Perlsteins for visa support again made me uneasy, but Pappa insisted. The opening of my letters had me worried, but I only wrote what is happening here. Pappa's friend, the Postmaster, passed his letters with the official Nazi censor stamp on it, so I know his aren't opened. We have also been lucky that my packages have not been gone through and items confiscated.

I was keeping up with the Olympics via our newspapers. We had not yet developed the coordinated professional teams and winter sports, as the Europeans had done. We were still too new at it, but the Summer Olympics would be great for the Americans.

The big excitement at school was a mysterious fire that was never explained. It gave us an unexpected three-day vacation. Unlike today, no one thought it as anything but an accident. Somehow the idea that it might have been set deliberately never occurred to us, as there seemed to be no problem children in our school. The ideal surroundings and the caring teachers made for stress-less learning. If there was any crime on the North Shore, it was an occasional theft, as there were enough well-off people to warrant it. In our household, Aunt Anne never wore extravagant jewelry, nor did the Perlsteins flaunt obvious wealth. If anything, it was quietly understated. Everything was in quiet good taste and spoke for itself. The publicity that surrounded many well-to-do families was shunned at our house. Aunt Anne would never publicize our trips, nor would she allow magazines like "House Beautiful" to feature the new home that was being built in Glencoe sometime in the coming year. Oh yes, we were to move again. This time into a custom designed new home on Sheridan Road in Glencoe.

March 30, 1936

Dear Little Thea,

Slowly we are coming out of winter, and the first greens of spring are poking through the earth. We hope you too are experiencing the rebirth of nature and a renewal of spirit. We're all well, thanks to G-d, and hope you are over all of your winter complaints, and as you say, "growing pains." Many young people are subject to them.

Since the end of January, our requests to emigrate are at the consulate, but we do not expect the bid before May or June. We simply have to be patient, as Job was.

The books you requested are packed and ready to go. There is so much leaving the house these days. Pesach is at hand, and I'm happy to say, we're able to get matzos from your uncle in Luxembourg. There is a nostalgic ritual about getting out the special Pesach dishes, packed in their white shrouded barrels, the burning of the last Chomitz, and all that the holiday signifies. With the Torah installed in our new living room and with a bottle of wine from Doctor Ludwig, the mayor, we shall have a proper celebration. I can never forget how, as a tiny girl, you used to crawl under the table during the long Seder and go to sleep at my feet. I wish I had a picture of that now.

Easter vacation will start soon, for you too, I imagine. Will you be getting a report card? I am waiting to read a copy of your report on Germany; perhaps it will create new interest to our dire situation.

There is a great deal of interest by your former teachers in your American grading system, and how you manage to get such good grades in a language not your own. I'm sure the "A" stands for the number "1" in our grading system, and so down the line. Am I correct? We're making progress in English, and I will send you my translation in another letter.

One more thing, as you learn to cook, do not forget to ask Mamma for some of her favorite recipes. She would be so thrilled and you will learn some fine cuisine. The Perlsteins' cook may enjoy them too. From the looks of you, she is feeding you very well.

With much love for today, Mamma and Lenchen are at their heavy Pesach cleaning, feather dusting and burning chomitz (leavened bread) and all that the ritual entails.

Your devoted Pappa

That time in my memory ...

The upbeat nature of Pappa's letter was reassuring, but still I felt guilty about all the space I was occupying. It was a bit unsettling as I reminded myself that, as a teenaged girl, I had nearly as much living area as my entire family back in Germany.

I was glad they got Matzos, although they didn't seem to be as important to me over here as they were at home. I spent the holiday with the Chicago relatives, as I had promised to do.

I do not recall that our household kept a strict Passover diet as there were so many non-Jews attached to it. The cook was Irish, a solid lady, given to no-nonsense and not much for French sauces. Fortunately I liked pot roast, corned beef, chicken and baked salmon. Her chocolate cake was out of this world, and so were all of her desserts. She was most generous in helping me with Grandmother's and Mamma's Alsatian and German Recipes which now found their way into our menus. The beauty of our kitchen was the input of international cooking in our meals. Tagne taught us how to make Finnish pastries; Karin brought us Swedish cookies and Apple Keevers; Aunt Anne's family filled us with Russian borscht and stuffed cabbage. There was no such thing as fast foods in those days. When we traveled by car there was always a "Dining with Duncan Hines" nearby. The age of McDonalds was yet to come.

18

April 1936

HEADLINES OF THE DAY:

VIENNA—Austria Violates 1919 Treaty of St. Germain, Reinstates Military Draft

NEW JERSEY—Lindbergh Kidnapper Bruno Hauptmann Executed

INDIA—Nehru Urges Socialism for India

GERMANY—Germans Who Failed to Vote for National Socialists Lose Jobs

NEW YORK—Admirers Storm Carnegie Hall for Arturo Toscanini's Farewell Performance with Philharmonic

April 12, 1936

Dear little Thea,

If we are late in replying to your letter of the 24th, you must blame it on the holidays. We were away and failed to make the ship schedule. Someday there will be a more speedy way to reach you, and since we cannot make telephone calls, this will have to do.

As I mentioned, Passover was reflective for all of us and at the end, instead of "next year in Jerusalem" we all prayed "next year in the U.S.A." where we can all celebrate together.

I am still having a bit of a problem with your explanation of the American grading system. You are not graded on specific holidays as our children are. And instead of 1, 2, 3 and 4, you receive A, B, C, and D (F). *Is that okay now?*[1]

Though we have been having spurts of spring weather, today, Easter Sunday, is a day of intermittent snow and rain. In spite of the bad weather the "Easter rabbit" brought many eggs and cakes (through the generosity of good neighbors). We have visitors from Erlenbach and so have some diversion. The Froehlichs received their immigration visa and, by my calculations, they were 4 to 6 months ahead of us. In your last letter you wrote the English sentence, "Please do not scold me for the short letter, but I have been busy catching up on everything because of my illness." As I translated it, was it correct? I hope so. But what was your illness?

Since all the relatives wish to write to you, I close with much love.

Your Pappa

That time in my memory ...

Every now and then, Pappa would slip in an English phrase. I also started to write more English in my letters, since my English vocabulary now seemed to outdistance my German one.

The traditional Passover/Easter exchange in Eisenberg still seemed to be in effect. For as long as I can remember, we exchanged Easter/Passover gifts with our neighbors. We would give them Matzos and Mamma's famous apple matzo Kugel and almond cake. In turn, on Easter, we would receive decorated eggs, chocolate rabbits, marshmallow chickens and whatever could be put into the ribbon-trimmed baskets we

---

1.   This sentence was set off in italics because Pappa originally wrote it in English.

would save from year to year. Sad to say, as I think about it now, there were no such exchanges in my new home. Oh, we had the standard supply of seasonal goodies. We were also invited to attend Easter egg hunts by Uncle Harry's business partners and their families. I remember a particularly festive one with the Shakman family. Jim Shakman was one of Uncle Harry's vice presidents. He and his wife Ann always included us in their celebration of the Christian holidays. The gifts that they presented to their twin nieces, whom they were raising, were duplicated in those they gave Betty Ann, Larry and me.

Then, too, my school friends and I were taken to a festive lunch and Easter show in downtown Chicago—Marshall Fields, of course. And there were new outfits for everybody in the family. Mine was a bright green with violets all over it and since that was my favorite flower, I adored it!

As a reward for every A and B I got, I could have a friend join us, so there were eight of us at luncheon and the movie, "The Story of Louis Pasteur", was an inspiring film for us to see as an example of public service. As I recall now, everything was done to insure my upbringing as a young lady with a mission in life. There were no slipshod experiments allowed.

April 15, 1936

Dear little Thea,

Our little signs of spring are already over and winter has set in again, but we must deal with the setbacks as well as the advances. That is the way life is. Luckily you, in your youth, do not have to deal with too many setbacks.

I have been away again on business, but I do miss the store. On the other hand, I could not have kept it going alone as the new law forbids anyone under 40 years of age to work for Jews in any capacity. Frau Kemp still helps me with bookkeeping, and that is a blessing. You write of moving again, to a bigger, brand new house; that all the children could draw what they would like in the new house is confusing, but send me your picture of what you would wish the new house to look like. I cannot imagine anything more beautiful than what you have now. Your foster parents must have their reasons for moving again. Will you be changing schools once more, or can you continue where you are?

Mamma will send you recipes as soon as she can. She has been having migraine headaches ever since the rebuilding of the house started. We are fortunate to have the apartment we do and were not relocated to some other unidentified place. You know they now have something called "relocation camps" opened for Hitler's coming birthday. They are to settle Jews to get ready for an exodus to Palestine, but I have my doubts that this will ever happen.

I must write all the relatives today, so this letter is short, but not without love. You know how much joy we gather from your happiness.

Until your next letter—

Your loving Pappa

That time in my memory ...

As I have mentioned before, we were again planning to move, this time into a home built especially for the family. The children could draw pictures of what we wanted in our rooms. I went overboard with built-in desk, bookcases, and my own bathroom. I would have loved an Erker (bay window) but that did not fit in with the house plans. To my knowledge the modern house was designed by the Pareira Brothers, who also designed sets for Paramount Pictures. The house was planned for a beautiful spot in Glencoe, Illinois. It was to have 6 bedrooms, each with its own bath, and every other type of room that would make for gracious living. One of the big attractions was a sweeping staircase, which was Aunt Anne's vision for the descent of her girls as brides:

And so it actually happened for me in 1946 when I became the bride of 1LT Harry Lindauer. The central round hallway opened to a small paneled library on the left, an oval dining room with English hunting scene murals overlooking the lake beyond that. Next to it, a small round breakfast room with direct access to the kitchen. Behind the two-story entrance hall, there was a half oval screened porch, also with a view of the lake. A large sunken living room stretched the entire width of the house on the right. Beyond that there was a tiled terraced sunroom with French doors. There was to be an elevator and grand ballroom on the third floor that could accommodate at least 150 people for a recital or dance. There was a pool, a fish pond, a tennis court and a four-car garage, with an apartment above it. The servants' quarters could accommodate five live-ins, with their own dining and living room. I am describing this house in detail, for a few years ago, it was considered the highest priced property on the North Shore.

From the groundbreaking on we took movies of the building progress every week. It was all very exciting to see it take shape. I could hardly concentrate on my schoolwork during that time.

My report on Germany was almost finished and my teacher looked forward to presenting it at graduation, and so did I. Pappa had sent me propaganda material, but to offset it, I talked about the children, who for one reason or another were taken from their parents for re-education. I particularly referred to children of Quakers, Mormon, or Fundamentalist parents, children who became wards of the state, totally removed from their parents' influence and religious beliefs. How different from my own condition! I hated to leave my friends in Highland Park, but then I had to leave so many of them, so often, so many other times. Still making new friends has been my salvation and pleasure all my life.

April 27, 1936

Dearest Daughter,

We finally received your letter from the ninth of April and want to answer it immediately. We are concerned about your strep throat, tonsillitis, and bad cold which forced you to take to your bed. Mrs. Perlstein's note is most reassuring, and Ruth and I were able to translate it most satisfactorily.

In spite of everything, we had a beautiful Passover with plenty of matzos and good food, thanks to our still loyal friends. Did you keep the holidays, too, or is that something only in your past? I realize being ill, you cannot concentrate on many things like writing to us, but you will bounce back and be your old self again before long. Think of all the reading and radio listening you can do. I am glad your big dog is such a good companion and that he is so attentive.

Ruth started school again and has your old teacher, Mr. Hein. He remembers you so well and is pleased to have Ruth in his class. We are fortunate that she can continue school.

Up to now, we have heard nothing from the consulate in Stuttgart, but we must be patient. We know that notification will come one day. I am certain of it. Your cousin Max from Schwegenheim will stop by on his business tour to pick us up for a little vacation with his parents. It will do us all good as the weather is again cold and wet. Yet, miraculously the almond trees are in bloom. We have never been more aware of the moods of nature until now.

Since you are ill, I'm sure you missed the Annweiler relatives who were in Chicago, but I am sure you will have other opportunities. I appreciate your drawing of what your new house in Glencoe will look like. You are right: The architect's drawing of this one is even more beautiful than the other two houses. It is a "real Hollywood setting", as you put it. You see, now you don't have to go there after all! How strange, we are both waiting to move into new quarters, but how different they are. We will find out more about your move, I am sure, and you will let us know the new address as soon as possible.

I am glad to hear that you can finish the year in your old school and start your new high school in the fall. Meanwhile, there is a long summer ahead for learning and exploring.

I shall write to Uncle Herman who decided to settle in Amsterdam where it is safer. He now realizes having you come to live with them was not such a good idea after all. Please forgive Mamma for not writing; her migraines are really bad these days. I am sure that she will feel better in new surroundings.

With much love from us all—

Your devoted Pappa

That time in my memory ...

It seems that with my growing anxieties I became more prone to minor illnesses. The worries about Mamma's migraines made my discomfort almost empathetic. I developed a thyroid condition that made for rapid weight gain and really drained my energies. My comfort, when I had to stay at home with the various infections, was reading. I must have read every young girl's book available at the time, plus any magazines that came to the house. Aunt Anne would bring me a beautiful breakfast tray and, as busy as she was, would start her day with an encouraging chat. The fact that the doctor came to the house made me feel important. The radio and its "romantic" soap operas made it a never-never land.

A note about Uncle Herman: He tried to persuade my father to let me come and live with his family. They left Luxembourg, moving to Amsterdam where they joined a thriving refugee community. However, Uncle Herman and his entire family perished in the first Nazi air attacks on that city. I feel as if I had a miraculous escape and thanked Pappa again for his foresight. It is something that continued to guide me all my life.

19

May 1936

HEADLINES OF THE DAY:

PALESTINE—Arabs Bar Jewish Entry into Palestine; 11 Die in Confrontations

BERLIN—Nazis Arrest 275 Monks for Practice of "Immorality" for Defying New Nazi Religious Doctrine

ROME—Mussolini Vows 400,000 Italians Will Stay in Ethiopia as Settlers; Proclaims Himself "Emperor"

AUSTRIA—Chancellor Schusschnigg Consolidates Control Over Austria; Strips Nazi Sympathizers of Political Power

UNITED STATES—German Dirigible Hindenburg Arrives in Lakehurst on First Transatlantic Flight

ENGLAND—Liner Queen Mary Sets Out on Maiden Voyage

May 6, 1936

Dearest little Thea,

Just as our letter of last week was sent off, your letter of the 17th of April arrived. Today is a big mail day, as letters are coming in from everywhere. I feel like Ezra, the scribe. Aunt Augusta and Uncle Julius wrote of meeting you in Chicago and were full of joy having done so. Your letter, surprisingly, never mentioned it and I wonder why, as it was truly so important for all of us.

For *Shavuoth*[1] we are again invited by the Monzernheimer relatives. This, once more, will be a diversion for us from all our latest problems.

Do you remember Mr. Herz, who lives in Frankfurt? He was our host every time we went there and remembers you and your first trip to the opera, "Hansel and Gretel." That night, he was sure you would become an opera singer, as you sang all the way home. He sends you much love and luck in your new home.

We finally have spring in all its splendor and people are moving to the outdoors again. Do you remember the wonderful children's parade with the long sticks and banners with ribbons and flowers and huge pretzels and apples on top? You paraded through the streets in pretty dresses singing Spring songs. Now it means a lot of folk marches and out-of-doors propaganda spectacles. I am sure it is very beautiful where you are with peace and serenity all around you. We really hope you are over your illness and can enjoy it all.

We still haven't heard from Stuttgart, so we do not expect to be interviewed before August or September. That means we cannot hope to leave here before next year. Hope is exactly what we are living on from day to day. I am still making the rounds of old customers in the outlying farms and villages, fulfilling their needs with what I can get from Uncle Herman who has been a good supplier, since there are still some goods available from his store in Heusweiler. No one seems to be concerned about our farmers, except that they are ordered to grow more and more food. With all their sons in either the S.A.[2] or the S.S.[3]—that is hard to do. Strangely enough, there are some young Jews now

---

1. Spring holiday of Thanksgiving
2. The S.A. or Sturmabteilung (Storm Detachment) was the Nazi's original paramilitary arm. Its members wore distinctive brown shirts and provided the "muscle" and organization for Nazi demonstrations, assaults on political rivals, and other political chores. Feared as a rival organization to the German Army, the S.A. was largely marginalized on June 30, 1934, when Hitler and his SS, in a massive and well-coordinated series of attacks, murdered or imprisoned the SA hierarchy, including its leader Ernst Röhm—Hitler's former commanding officer.

working on these farms and feeling much safer and well protected—if that is possible in this uncertain age.

We hope your next letter will tell us what your summer plans are, whether or not you will be returning to your camp or travel somewhere else.

For today we send all our love—

Your devoted Pappa.

That time in my memory ...

Yes, I remembered the May parades with beautiful flowers and banners, with huge pretzels and apple-decorated sticks signifying the end of the school year. They were as much of a tradition as the May baskets that mean so much to me today. Again, so varied are the remembrances: When serving overseas in later years, the First of May meant retreating into a military American compound to avoid the confrontations of a May Day communist parade.

The move of some young Jews to farmlands of Germany surprised many families, but it kept them out of the factories and labor camps. Somehow, it also made them feel safer. This eventually stopped when the government started sending girls of questionable character to work at these farms. Ironically, their reputation was the worst; they were prostitutes and thieves. Still, the government would not expose them to the propositions of a possible "Rasenschänder", a man of non-Aryan blood who would dare seek a relationship with a German Fraülein, no matter how bad her reputation was.

Some Jews who still had some money did invest in farmland as did my Uncle Herman, to secure a safer place for the family and produce food for them. But then he made the ill-advised move to Amsterdam.

On this side of the ocean, I entered into my confirmation training year, as it was customary in Reform Judaism. It gave me a whole set of new responsibilities. Even the children were in awe and shared their treats much more readily as they looked on me

---

3.   The S.S. or Schutzstaffel (Protection Squadron) grew out of Hitler's personal body-guard to become a powerful and feared organization with its own uniforms, ranks, training camps, and leadership. Headed by Heinrich Himmler, the S.S. wore stark black uniforms. During World War II the S.S. became a virtual army outside the Wehrmacht—it numbered over 100,000 men, accepted "Nordic" recruits from nations as diverse as Norway, Croatia, and the Ukraine, and enforced fanatical discipline on its members. It also ran the vast Nazi concentration camp system.

as being almost grown-up. I looked forward to being finished with the dentist and having my braces come off in time for my confirmation the following year. It was really something to anticipate.

May 29, 1936

My dear Thea,

As usual we take such pleasure from your letters—a real lifeline of hope. In the last few days we had many letters from America which I must answer immediately, as they concern our visa application. One is from Uncle Julius in St. Charles who hopes to be able to help us. He has made excellent connections. Patience is our byword; so far G-d has granted me that.

The weather is considerably warm for this time of year, and Ruth has taken advantage of it by swimming. We delight in our cool bathtub, as even the pleasure of swimming in the lake has been taken from us. We're glad that Ruth's loyal girlfriends can smuggle her in. Such simple pleasures in life are so important.

Once more you will be going to your camp after a family vacation on the Michigan shores. I hope it is a reward for your hard schoolwork. With all the subjects you are taking, English is the one I would like to listen in the most. How much there is to learn!

I am writing you my translation as you wrote it. "Daddy" I presume is the affectionate word for Pappa, I know "father" is the formal one. "Your loving daughter" is one I had no problem translating. You apparently don't want to be called "little daughter" or "little Thea" anymore. Very well, I shall do that. I sometimes forget that you are growing up physically and socially, as well as intellectually. The phrase "in case" I am having trouble translating. How is it used? You must be patient with me: at my age it is not so easy to learn a new language. Even Gerda writes me in English now.

A word about your wonderful drawings of the new house. Again, it is beautiful as in a fantasy. To create something that beautiful is a real gift of G-d. The buildings built here have no heart and soul; they are erected for the glory of the Third Reich and look impressive, but cold: Even the private homes must conform to an accepted party standard. Many towns have standard models of homes and you can pick A, B, or C for your residence. They are built in the old Teutonic style, very picturesque but in many cases outmoded. The brilliant architects of our time have all emigrated to the United States.

For today we send all our love. Mamma begs to be excused: she is getting ready for a visit from more relatives.

With deep affection—Your "Daddy"

That time in my memory ...

As I began writing more English, "Daddy" replied in kind, but the bulk of our correspondence remained in German. I knew writing in English takes away some of the anxiety about the Visas and was another sign of continued hope. Pappa really made a momentous effort to learn English, as did the rest of the family. It really rekindled their hopes of emigration. I sent a picture of word games, such as the ones that teach very young children. They helped identify words but did not help with the grammar. That is why children find it so much easier to learn—they don't worry so much about the correctness of grammar but attack a subject with enthusiasm.

As our house progressed, I became more and more aware of the freedom and beauty of its functional design and the difference between it and the restrictive architecture of the new Germany. Here the architects dared to use new materials, open designs related to nature. No wonder Walter Gropius[4] and Mies Van der Rohe[5] were ecstatic about designing in the USA.

I really looked forward to giving my report on German children at the graduation from 8th grade, and wondered what would be ahead of me that summer.

---

4.   Walter Gropius (1883-1969) was the creator of the *Bauhaus* School of architecture and one of the 20th Century's most influential architects. From 1915 to 1920 he was the second husband of Alma Mahler, widow of the noted composer. Alma's third husband was Franz Werfel, until his death in 1945.

5.   Ludwig Mies van der Rohe (1886-1969) was also associated with the *Bauhaus* School. After coming to the United States, he designed some of Chicago's most striking and elegant buildings.

Flower Address

FLOWER ADDRESS
written by Thea Kahn
for Confirmation, 1936

Have you ever thought what could be the largest garden in this world? Who is its great keeper? Its flowers are numerous in growth and also variety. They receive their nourishment from many sources and in most cases used it throughout their entire life. The keeper of the garden is a master of his art. He is kind and generous to his good flowers, firm and punishing to the bad ones; he shows pity for the unfortunates and mercy to the humble ones.

Could there be a greater garden than the earth and a better keeper than this eternal God? The flowers are we ourselves. Some of us grow in good and prosperous lives and others in ill-fated existence. Our nourishment is the knowledge of religion and the general problems of living. We receive all this from the Temple and our homes.

We have flowers on the surface of this earth that have grown wild for a great period of their lives. A gardener planted some in good soil, took good care of them and so raised beautiful flowers. The human being is no exception from the wonders of nature. Some of our great leaders in Judaism were born in parts of a country where standards of living were low. But God gave them strength and will-power and made them famous men.

As we stand here on this, our Confirmation Day, we have been transplanted from the circle of the younger flowers to the world of the adults. We must realize most of our playing days are over and that we must start to plant our roots deeper in the ground of serious life.

So, the youth of today, have a great future lying before us and are ready for responsibility put on our shoulders. We cannot entirely follow the footsteps of our forefathers because the standards of civilization have changed since their days.

As the flowers have to live through a time of good and bad days, we also have to find a way through clouds of doubt and disillusionment. But like a good gardener protects his flowers, the God of Israel will lead us from our rough path of misfortune to the light.

And now as we stand in this house of worship, we give all our thanks to God for His guidance through the childhood of our lives. May our belief in Him help us along through the dark days ahead as it helped our ancestors years ago.

Through the great Lord's divine help we hope to reach our goal, and, as we start on our journey, let us strew the glorious flowers of love, truth and courage. Let us, too, carry the torch of Judaism through the passage of the future. Amen.

20

June 1936

ROME—Italy Conquers Ethiopia. "Italy At Last Has Her Empire", Boasts Mussolini

GERMANY—Historian Oswald Spengler Dies in Exile; Rejected Nazi Racial Theories

MADRID—36 Churches Burned in 48 Hours

BERLIN—Himmler named Head of Reich Police

NEW YORK—German Boxer Max Schmeling KOs Joe Louis in 12th Round

PHILADELPHIA—FDR and John Garner Nominated on Democratic Presidential Ticket

June 3, 1936

Dear little Thea,

By the time you get this letter, you will have begun your confirmation year. The speech you wrote is beautiful, and I shall treasure it always close to my heart. It was thoughtful of you to send, not only the English copy, but also to translate it into German. The English copy will certainly help me with my studies. You call it the Flower Address, the most important speech of the occasion. I'm sure it will be a great honor to deliver it. As for your confirmation itself, like a Bat Mitzvah, you will step into the circle of adults. Keep that in mind, and remember that you have responsibilities to fulfill, not that you have been unaware of them, ever since we sent you abroad. Your foster parents will be as proud of you as we are.

Your letter reached us in Monzernheim, and we were delighted to read it to the relatives, particularly about the wonderful party you were given in the anticipation of the event scheduled for next year. They could hardly believe the festivities as you described them. It did us all so much good to know that there are such giving people in the world. It made our disappointing visit to the consulate more bearable. Again, our visas were denied on grounds that there was not enough security guaranteed; not enough support pledged. They feel that with my age and my eye problems, my ability to work would be handicapped. They don't know me. As yet, I still do not want you to ask the Perlsteins to pledge for us, but I will ask both uncles, Julius and Ernest, to stand up for our future support. In spite of it all, we are still optimistic that a way will be found; it may take just a little more patience.

We are glad that you are able to pursue your beloved sports again. Here, all the Jewish athletes—and there are many of them—are not allowed to compete in the Olympic Games, although they did admit several American Jews under pressure. Just remember, sports are wonderful, but don't let the intense training push the joy of learning into the background: One is as important as the other. The fact that you received a blue and red ribbon for your riding should not detract from the joy of receiving A's and B's on your report card.

The excitement and dread about my going to court in Kirchheimbolanden all came to naught, as I could prove with my good friends' pledges that my earnings were within the dictates of the existing laws. So much for justice of the land, and the words of dedicated friends. I don't know who denounced me, but may he sleep in peace.

For today, with love and kisses—Your Dad

P.S. I shall be traveling again, so no letter next week.

That time in my memory ...

Once again Uncle Ernest's affidavit declaration was not financially large enough to vouch for the family's income, should they come to the States. The fear of "going on welfare" was always a question in the recession-riddled government agenda. Father's age and physical condition, particularly regarding his cataracts may also have been factors of his concern. He was already in his 50s.

The big event I was preparing for was conformation in the coming year. Confirmation, unlike Bar or Bat Mitzvah introduced the older (15 years of age) child into the Covenant. It was a ceremony observed strictly by Reform Jews. The fact that it took a year of preparation made it very significant for me, and that I was given the honor of the "Flower Address" brought great joy. My mentors were Rabbi and Mrs. Charles Shulman—a great influence in my life at that time. The fact that I was given the flower address for the following years confirmation, took the sting out of what to me was a rather embarrassing incident.

I was on my way to go sailing with my friends on the family catamaran, when Aunt Anne reminded me to be back punctually for a 6 o'clock dinner. She was having some guests and there was to be a young people's table where all the children would gather. To my frustration and chagrin, the wind died down on our return trip, and I barely had time to brush my hair and add a skirt to my middie blouse. Barreling into the dining room where everyone was already seated, I sputtered out an apology, adding "we were necking all the way home to get here on time, since the wind had died down." Aunt Anne gasped and so did everyone else, while her table partner chuckled and said," I think the young lady means they tacked all the way home." Looking bewildered, I nodded my head—not quite knowing what I had said wrong. In German the word for moving with the wind is "Halsen"—"Hals" being the neck. Therefore it seemed logical to say necking. Sailors call it tacking. I took my place with the young people, who were all snickering, and a cool 15 year old informed me that "necking" is something you do in a rumble seat when you're "making out." I wanted to sink into the floor with embarrassment. Aunt Anne's look said "don't you dare leave the table," and with that she told everyone about my being chosen for the flower address at the following confirmation. That and the fact that I got a special award in English, at grammar school graduation saved my bruised ego.

I was at the end of my Grammar School education and looked forward to high school in the fall. My report on German children, as part of the graduation ceremony, was well-received, and brought me a special award in English. Sadly, I had to say good-bye to my schoolmates, as they were going on to Highland Park High School while I was to enter New Trier in Winnetka. It was considered one of the finest and innovative high schools in the country. I had chosen it in preference to a private country day school, which seemed too confining. I was fascinated by the idea of going to New Trier, because Pappa came from Old Trier, a town on the Moselle River in Germany. It felt like an omen.

Gerda's letter from Bremen:

June 4, 1936

My dear sister Thea,

At last I am able to write you. I've had the intention so often and then postponed it again and again. Perhaps I felt that my own house should be in order before I tackled the problems of others (that's the psychiatrist in me). My work with Dr. Buchholz is very demanding, but rewarding. It gives me the solace I so desperately need after my traumatic divorce. Just remember: It was the orders of the government that changed all our lives, not the feelings of individuals. I know Wolfgang loves all of us dearly.

Now that I have made a beginning, I hope you come back with a long explicit letter of all that is going on in your life. It must be a tremendous upheaval, because life in the U.S.A. is so different. I needn't ask you how you like it: your enthusiastic letters certainly show it, but aren't you sometimes a little nostalgic and homesick, if not for Germany itself, then certainly for us who love you? I think of you so often: What a brave and spirited little girl you are! Don't ever lose that spirit, and you will achieve what you set out to do. I wonder what kind of a career you picture for yourself; have you made any plans? I know you always dreamed of being with Wolfgang and me, studying medicine in Leipzig. Are these still your intentions in the U.S.A.? At this point in time you seem much more in love with the arts. Your enthusiasm for learning will open so many fields. Are you still writing regularly to the parents? I hope you do, because they live for your letters so desperately. You probably heard that their visa was denied again, but we are all hopeful that another attempt will succeed. Once they are in the U.S.A. I will join you all, and we will be together again as a family.

I get out very seldom. I don't really enjoy being in company, but when I have free time I get on my bicycle and take off into the countryside, where it is peaceful and quiet. Then too, I do a lot of swimming. Unfortunately it is still cold, even for June, but summer is just beginning. I swim in the Weser River where it is a bit warmer than in the ocean. At *Whitsuntide*[1] I took a trip to the island Helgoland. To sail on the ocean was a delight. I wasn't seasick one moment, and the village on the island was sparkling with its miniature houses and flower gardens. It was just at a time for a sailing regatta, and I enjoyed it with a group of young tourists. The world and politics seemed far away. We swam in the cold ocean, but didn't mind it a bit. I got very tan, even in a short

---

1.   Summer Solstice

time. You would have thought I had vacationed for at least two weeks. Sad to say, I cannot contact them once we're back in Germany. It would be too complicated, as my Aryan name only belies my status.

But now I have a lot of questions for you. Please open your heart to me; I know there is a lot you cannot share with the parents. You are growing into a young woman, and I really cannot call you little sister anymore. You will have all the joys and anxieties of growing up. I hope you miss all the depressions that accompany it. What about your friends, are they both boys and girls? You may write me anything and it will be only between us. As your big sister, studying in the psychiatric field, I hope I can give you good advice. When you are alone among strangers, it is good to have someone familiar and close where you can pour out your heart.

So my dear sister-growing-up, write soon, and continue to enjoy all that is around you, and continue to study as you have been doing. Stay well and remember your big sister

Gerda

P.S. Don't forget my new address. As you can see I'm keeping my married name, it makes things easier.

That time in my memory …

I did open up with my anxieties to Gerda, but avoided the questions about career plans. I did not want to upset her with my decision not to try for a medical career. I was more interested in the arts and always have been, as my life today bears out. I admired the way she kept her life going, taking the opportunities as they came along.

She, of course, was right, I did miss my family—the easy relationships we had. I loved my new family but not in the same way. I was more on guard more aware of the burden of responsibility not to disappoint them. The determination to do well at school blotted out many fears and anxieties about the family, but not always. The contrast between my life and theirs was too great. It made me an "old" child. It kept me from participating in some of the activities that unthinking children do like Halloween tricks and Fourth of July setting off firecrackers.

Gerda's divorce really saddened me, because we all loved her husband dearly. Whenever he came to visit with her, he brought magic to the house. He brought me my first taste of Ovaltine and puffed rice, besides fruit-flavored vitamins and foods that are now part of our daily lives, but were then in experimental stages. These were all part of the nutritional experiments in which Wolfgang participated.

To this day, I do not know what sort of deal he made with the German govern-ment to keep Gerda out of a concentration camp and eventually let her continue her medical studies in Brazil.

June 10, 1936

Dear Thea,

As you are studying for your confirmation, I am reluctant to call you little Thea. You now will have adult responsibilities. We had letters from everywhere, so this will be a big writing day. Since I love doing that, it will be a pleasurable day for me.

We are happy to hear that you did well on your school exam and finished up elementary school in fine shape. I know you earned yourself a fine vacation and will be glad to see your campmates from last year. No doubt you look forward to all your favorite sports. Here we have an unlikely summer, much too cold and rainy to be outside. I'm sorry for the young people who have to march, rain or shine, for the Olympics, for the glory of the Fatherland. Even as far away as we are from Berlin, we have foreign visitors, so all the streets are spruced up and flags are flying. Every town is like a stage setting. Only we see the artificiality of it: International visitors see only the glory and pageantry, but none of the underlying tension and tyranny.

Max again picked us up for a visit with his parents—another little diversion we need badly. We are awaiting your big picture portrait of your graduation and the celebration of your presentation on German children. Let us know more about the high school you will be attending. With much love and greetings from the relatives and to all who take care of you.

Your Pappa, "Dad"

That time in my memory ...

Graduation from grammar school was a fairly quiet event, as we were a small group. It was the first time I had met some of my classmates' parents. The dignity of the occasion was worthy of a high school graduation, with a send-off party for the children. Since I was the only one going to a different high school, I did not quite share the enthusiasm of the others. There was a family celebration that night with all the Perlstein-Agazim relatives but although my Chicago family was invited, they did not attend. They seemed reluctant to share this beautiful setting with me. However, I was allowed to invite some of my classmates, and their families which made it even more special for me.

The Olympics were in full preparation all over Germany: Even the smallest of villages had an Olympic committee. Anti-Semitism was toned down somewhat, but none of the German-Jewish sports clubs, even those with superb athletes, were allowed to participate in the games.

Ruth's letter:

June 10, 1936

Dear Thea,

Do you know I can't sleep? Dear Mamma will take me to Dr. Neumann in Grün-stadt to find out the reason. I know already. It's because I worry a lot; I will be old and gray before my time. It isn't as much fun anymore since you are gone. Your girlfriends ask about you when no one's around. Only the teachers ask out in the open and the Catholic sisters. Only one of the old ones is left, and she always reminds me I cannot do my Handarbeit (knitting crocheting and embroidery) as good as you did. Thank you for the picture; you look so serious: Don't you smile anymore? Is it because of your braces? At first I thought it was a dollar but since it didn't have a picture of the president on it, I decided it must be you. JUST JOKING!! I'm waiting for the package you promised; I hope it has chocolate in it. I still have a few "Baby Ruth" chocolates from before, and I don't like to waste them. How do you like my English script? I'm one of the few girls who is allowed to learn it. The others all write ordinary German. (Please turn the page)

Did you notice I said "Dear Thea" instead of "Theachen?" I think it's silly when you are growing up to be called little Thea or little Ruth. You don't write much about the boys you meet. I would love to meet some nice boys, but they are all afraid or too stuck up to talk to me. I don't know who it is, but someone puts daisies on my desk sometimes. I still visit the relatives, and that is much fun. Max takes us everywhere. He is very handsome, and I think he has a German girlfriend, but nobody says anything about it. It could get him into a lot of trouble.

Write me about all the presents you get. The sweater you sent me is getting too small, as I am growing "you-know-where." It's nice you can still knit. I wish I had a bicycle like yours. Mine is nice enough for the time being.

As long as my knees don't hit the handlebars, I'll be all right. The youth group master doesn't like the kids to ride, but march all the time. I'm excused because I'm Jewish: Aren't I lucky? I hope you know this is a long letter, because I love you. I have to go to bed now, 'ugh.' The nursery has a mouse. I can hear it scratching when the lights are out. I suppose it wants company, too. I send you hugs and kisses.

Your sister, Ruth.

That time in my memory ...

Ruth's letter eased much of the worry, as I rediscovered the little imp in her. It does not seem to have suffered too much under the deprivation she was experiencing. My guilt feelings were more on her account than anyone else's.

So far, she still had the staunch support of some of her teachers, some classmates and, of course, the nuns of the Parish. Since our former nursemaid became a nun, and Mamma supported their order, Ruth was a favorite there.

Meanwhile, I was getting ready for a cloudless summer of swimming at Michiana Shores and camp afterwards. Then, too, there was the prospect of high school in the fall, and that was very exciting. I had received a copy of my proposed schedule, and was to be tested for an "X" (Experimental Class) program. It was something new for the school, and I looked forward to this challenge. Some of the instruction, especially in the arts, was W.P.A. sponsored and involved artists, actors, musicians and all those who had difficulty maintaining living wages during those depression-ridden times. Again, the prospects of new friends, new opportunities made me eager for fall to come.

June 14, 1936

Dear daughter Thea,

As you can see I am now aware of your growing adult status, particularly since you graduated elementary school. It seems strange, for many of our children; it is the end of formal education, unless they want to learn a trade. For you it is only the beginning. Have you decided what you want to have as a career? You haven't mentioned medicine in a long time. From all the lessons you are having, no doubt, it will be something in the arts. That is fine too. It is so sad that many of our respected artists, writers, and musicians can no longer create in Germany. They are taking their gifts elsewhere, to the United States most emphatically. The celebration at your graduation sounded so beautiful and caring, a real family party. I should hope you will thank everyone for the many gifts you have received and, if I may repeat, show them you are truly worth of all their attentions.

Let us hear when you move into the new house. With camp and summer vacation ahead, I expect our letter writing to be more erratic; less often. Nonetheless, it will be as affectionate as ever.

Wishing you a wonderful summer—

Your devoted father

That time in my memory ...

As I began writing more in English, "Daddy" replied in kind. The bulk of our correspondence, however, remained in German. I knew his writing in English would take away some of the anxiety about the visa turndowns, and was another sign of continuing hope.

I looked ahead to summer and all the activities it offered, the lakeshore in Michigan and, after that, Camp Burr Oaks. I was allowed to have two camp mates share our Michigan vacation with the family and was delighted at the prospect. The question was, which ones, as I loved all of them equally. I chose a friend from Omaha, Nebraska, since I would be visiting her on winter vacation and one from Winnetka, who would become my best friend in high school. The excitement of rescue from a capsized sailboat on Lake Michigan became the highlight of our vacation experience, one that labeled us heroines all through camp. That part of my summer adventure I kept from the family, they had enough to worry about.

June 24, 1936

Dear Daughter,

This is a very quick note to let you know that, for the first time in many months, we had an inquiry as to your well-being from the committee of HIAS. Apparently the agency is now in Berlin, and there seemed to be a lack of communication on their part. I have the feeling they no longer send as many children abroad as before. Some of the children apparently did not have the wonderful experiences you have had, though that is to be expected. The main thing is that they are out of this country and safe. But they do their best in very trying circumstances. It is a wonderful organization, along with the others who concern themselves so genuinely with your well-being.

We are sending Ruth on an extensive trip to the relatives. Apparently someone complained, and she no longer can swim in the lake with her little friends. What harm can swimming by such a little girl do to upset the race balance of the Third Reich? Anyway, the prospective trip has taken her mind off this minor tragedy, and she is anxious to start and be able to compare her summer with you. Don't forget to give us your changes of address.

In Haste—Your loving Daddy

That time in my memory ...

It was good that the prospect of a visit to the relatives brightened Ruth's summer. I felt I was becoming accident-prone. Every time Daddy wrote of some restriction or tightening of the law, I seemed to have some mishap—the last being an ankle infection after a fall from my horse. It might have kept me off the horses at camp that summer.

Imagine an adult writing an order, on official stationary, with an imposing seal, just to keep a little girl out of a swimming hole! I was very upset that Ruth couldn't go swimming anymore, and angry at my friends for not protecting her more. In retrospect, there was no way that children could protest anything with an official seal on it.

HIAS, the Hebrew Immigrant Aid Society, was suddenly swamped with requests for children's transport out of Germany by anxious parents. Many had contacted Pappa after my successful emigration to the United States, but all he could do for them was to refer them to the agency. Unbeknownst to him, it had relocated to Berlin and contacted him about my well-being from there. Children were still leaving Germany in a steady stream, but not all of them through HIAS. There were many independent agencies and church groups who helped. The Quakers of Philadelphia were one such group. Others now on the rescue roster were The American Friends Service, The American Jewish Committee, American Jewish Congress, American Jewish Joint Distribution Committee, B'nai B'rith, B'rith Sholom, and The National Council of Jewish Women.

Well-to-do families from all over America made a tremendous effort. One such family rescued 50 children from Austria. I can't imagine the organizations losing interest in the children, but a lack of interest developed in Congress and the project was abandoned. The plan of rescuing 20,000 children was voted down and eventually abandoned.

As the research of Iris Posner and her committee proved, there were barely 1000 children* who emigrated under these organizations' auspices. All of this came to light in the past few years.

* Now The Thousand Children Incorporated.

June 30, 1936

Dear daughter Thea,

Today's mail was quite heavy with questions about how to get the children out of the country. It is hard to answer them, since you wrote that the people in Congress are no longer supportive of the program, and that the bill admitting 20,000 children to the United States was turned down. I don't understand it—the need is more urgent now than it was when you left. I will write the committee in Berlin about starting it up again to get more children to safety. We still have not received the big portrait you promised. Elsie also writes she has not heard from you. Is something wrong? You wrote about falling off the horse: Is everything all right. Mrs. Perlstein's note reassured us considerably as to your injury.

Thanks to Max we had a beautiful tour of the Karlsberg Woods. We gathered pinecones and blueberries which Mamma will put to good use this winter. That is our recreation and will revive our lagging spirits come winter.

You have your long summer vacation ahead, presumably at camp again. Be careful that you don't overdo it; I know you are very competitive. Perhaps some indoor activity would also be beneficial.

All of Germany is spruced up for the Olympic Games. With athletes from all over the world, the big talk is about an American Negro runner, Jesse Owens, who is supposed to be the fastest man on Earth. We all hope he will prove that. It would really put an end to the Nazi-super-race theory. We keep hoping for miracles. Sad to say, there are so few these days. My friend the pastor admits there is very little Christian teaching and preaching these days. Even Pastor Niemöller[2] has become disillusioned.

So much for observing worldly philosophy! I hope someday you will understand it all and add to the betterment of the world.

Tonight we play a rummy game we have invented. It uses 106 cards and demands of a good memory. Ruth is almost always the first to go out and that pleases her immensely. She is even willing to go to bed in triumph afterwards. As a child she has so much to cope with—we are so proud of her. Have a wonderful summer, we will be writing and hope you will too.

Your affectionate family and Dad

---

2.   The chief spokesman for the Lutheran Church.

That time in my memory ...

Dad's reference to Olympic competitor Jesse Owens was certainly exciting news, which all the U.S. newspapers took full advantage of. Dad assessed the situation correctly. He could put an end to the claim of the German-super-race mentality.

America was able to send some Jewish athletes by pressuring the German government, but, as mentioned before, none of the German Jewish sports clubs were allowed to participate.

Pappa's mention of Pastor Niemöller referred to the remarks he finally made in his resistance to the Nazi regime: "—They came for the communists but I was not a communist ... so I did not speak ... They came for the labor unionists, but I was not a unionist ... so I did not speak. They came for the Jews but I was not a Jew ... So I did not speak. Then they came for me and there was no one to speak for me." He counts among the righteous Gentiles who spoke out and did not parrot the Nazi Doctrine or Racial Superiority and the total omission of the Old Testament from the present day Protestant belief.

21

July 1936

HEADLINES OF THE DAY:

GENEVA—Jewish Journalist Kills Himself at League of Nations Meeting to Protest German Treatment of Jews

GENEVA—League of Nations Abandons Ethiopia, Discontinuing Sanctions on Italy

UNITED STATES—Negro Jesse Owens Wins 2 Spots on U.S. Olympic Team

BERLIN—Hitler/Schusschnigg Sign Pact Conceding Austrian Independence

MADRID—Army Uprising in Morocco Spreads to Spain; Franco Lands with Troops

MADRID—Spain Orders Churches Confiscated, Decrees Government Control of Industry

UNITED STATES—Heat Wave Death Toll Reaches 3,000

LONDON—England Begins Mass Production of Gas Masks—One for Each Citizen

July 21, 1936

Dear Thea,

I was unable to answer your last two letters immediately as I was on an extended trip again and you know how Mamma hates to write without me. This time it included Wawern, where we met with Uncle Herman. He is disappointed with Luxembourg and will move to Amsterdam. So we said goodbye with deep emotions. G-d only knows when we shall meet again. He finally admitted it was wiser to send you across the ocean, than have you come and live with him and the family. He is still hoping to settle in Paris one day. The trip took me far afield as more and more people need passage to the U.S.A. The ships are fully booked.

In the meantime, you have had your fourteenth birthday and we know from the past it was well celebrated. I will answer your "English letter", by and by, as I'm caught up in so much letter writing. I could use a secretary. Ruth offered her new English handwriting, but I'm afraid she's just a little too small for such a strenuous task. At the moment she is saying goodbye to the Winkler family, who will settle in New York where another family member is in the restaurant business. It seems strange that even some of our Christian families want to leave, the Winklers being a case in point. Grandmother Winkler says that the last thing she wants is her dear Willy to become an arrogant Hitler Youth. I wish them much luck and wish we were already in their shoes.

I'm assuming camp is enjoyable and you're having a great reunion with last year's friends. You speak of being in a musical. What is a musical? It is like an opera? A play with music? Please explain further. What do you play?

It doesn't seem like summer. Although you are having record heat it is cool and overcast here, but even the weather does not curb the enthusiasm for the Olympics.

Don't get too involved in your sports program, so that you have no time to write and contemplate. Find yourself a quiet corner, the shade of a tree, somewhere where you have time to reflect, to read and write. Until we hear from you again, in the meantime we send all our love.

Your Daddy

That time in my memory …

At camp we produced another "Broadway musical." One of our counselors, a script writer, encouraged us to write it for parents' day. Today I still sing the lyrics to one of the songs to that show. It was called "Until Tomorrow." I remember it to this day. We always hoped it would be published, but it never was. Still, we all felt like stars on Broadway. It did inspire me to resume voice lessons in the fall.

As to the Olympics, they were still the news of the day and politics came secondary. The soft pedaling of Anti-Semitism and the restrictions on the German people was strictly a show case demonstration, but it made everyone breathe a little easier. Much to Mr. Hitler's embarrassment, but as predicted, Jesse Owens was the star of the games. His performances and his personal stature made him everybody's hero. Hitler, in great embarrassment, left the stadium, ostensibly because of threatening rain without congratulating Owens and other Negro medalists. He received the German medalist surreptitiously, so he would not have to acknowledge America's Negro and Jewish winners.

Letter from Gerda from Bremen:

July 29, 1936

My dear Sister,

You will be surprised that I write you an entire letter in English. That is your language now, and we should all practice it for the future. First of all, let me thank you for your thoroughly enjoyable letter. I am so glad that you are studying hard, but having a good time doing it. Your foster parents must be so wonderful by really including you in all their family life.

Perhaps I better switch to German again, where I can express myself more fully. I am surprised that you find Latin so boring. It is the basis of all studies and broadens the field for all that you do. With all that your foster parents approve in your extra activities, Latin should be one. I cannot express enough, that you are a clever thoughtful girl and can project what career opportunities are open to you. I beg of you to include Latin in your studies. Perhaps you can curtail one or two of your sports. While it is healthy and satisfying, sports alone cannot provide you with a secure future. I don't want to spoil your joy in all you do, merely to point out something you might miss later on. It is very nice that you are learning a great deal of English from good films. I too like the movies, but we do not have the excellent ones you can see, only those full of propaganda for the glory of the Third Reich. If I may suggest, go only once a week and save the money for your little sister Ruth. The poor child has so little joy. The children are afraid and reluctant to play with her. I sent her books and toys, you know Thea it would be a small sacrifice for you. Incidentally that is a very generous allowance your foster parents give to you; that they bank most of it for you is very wise. Do you realize there are family fathers all over the world who don't make that much money in a week? Don't ask the parents about sending something, they will say no. I say just send something that gives you pleasure and it will give Ruth double the joy.

I will switch to English again. Here in Germany, everything is geared for the Olympic Games. The streets of Bremen and every other city, town and village are decorated and painted. The Nazi rhetoric has been toned down so as not to shock all the visitors who come from all over the world. I can sit at a sidewalk café and hear all languages spoken around me. I have a hard time, not so much with French and Italian, but the English that is spoken too quickly. I hope I can manage that when I come to the United States. I hope I can travel soon, so I can work on this special subject. Who knows what time will bring me? My days are dark and heavy, and only God can help me, but like Pappa I believe in all things good.

Now I close since it was quite a strain to write in English. When I write again, perhaps it will become less difficult. So for today, I will close, wishing you all joy and well-being. There are so many questions only you can answer.

Your big sister—Gerda

That time in my memory ...

Gerda again wrote in her quaint English, only to switch to German halfway through and then back again. As always, we were at odds regarding what she considered a classic, university-preparing education. Again, the guilt feelings about squandering my allowance bothered me. What she does not realize is that spending some along with my friends was very important to me. I was allowed $5.00 out of the allowance that was banked for me for the future. This bought my lunches and a Saturday treat with my friends. I was very careful how I spent it, knowing the need at home. Pappa kept reassuring me they were provided for. The economics of the day, although on the rise, were still too low to benefit the average American. Even though, I seemed to live in the lap of luxury, it was never flaunted, as by some families in similar situations. As mentioned before, there was no ostentation in the Perlstein family. With all the luxury surrounding me, I was still responsible for the cleanliness of my room and closet, to keep check on my clothes and be generally helpful where needed. I will never forget Aunt Anne on the eve of an important party scrubbing a spill on the kitchen steps, because everybody had their duty and it had to be done here and now. She pointed out to me: "Never be ashamed to do honest work. You can't order others to do it, if you haven't done it yourself." It was an object lesson I never forgot. She was a modest but great lady.

22

August 1936

HEADLINES OF THE DAY:

BERLIN—Negro Athlete Jesse Owens Wins Four Gold Medals at Olympic Games

SPAIN—Franco Takes Badajoz, Uniting Rebel Fronts; Promises Liberal Regime

FRANCE—Premier Leon Blum Declares Non-Intervention in Spanish Civil War, Asks European Powers to Follow

GERMANY—Reichsminister Joachim von Ribbentrop Named Reich Envoy to Great Britain

GERMANY—Germany, Russia Ban Arms Exports to Spain

August 2, 1936

Dear little Thea,

Although we heard nothing from you for two weeks, we were blessed with two letters on Thursday and Friday. We were relieved to know that you are physically fine and your mishap with the horse had a happy ending. Meanwhile, your surprise birthday party at Michiana Shores sounded like great fun. Imagine friends coming all the way from Chicago to attend it. It must have been unusual, since everyone came in a bathing suit. Here we can't even think about swimming. There isn't a day without rain. I hope you are grateful and thank everyone for the lovely birthday presents you received. Stationery, radio, books, handkerchief—that all sounds proper for a young lady growing up. G-d willing I hope we can be at your next birthday party and add our gifts too.

Here the life cycle goes on: Some are born and some die. Sadly to say, many of my good friends are passing on. Ironically, they are the good Germans as well as the bad, God makes no distinction. Uncle Herman and family are settled in Amsterdam. We hope it was a good move, as the Dutch are friendly and sympathetic, and many refugees have landed there.

We're about to go on another long circuit of goodbyes, as well as helping the relatives bring in their harvest. At least we shall have food for the winter. Many people won't, in spite of the glowing reports by the government. With so many young men going away from home in the S.A. or S.S. it leaves only the old men to work the farms. They are now sending young girls from the cities, some with questionable backgrounds, to help out, but since they considered it a form of punishment, it does not work very well. They stopped sending Jewish young people and now send them to labor camps and "controlled" factories, meaning war industry. Ruth is very excited about the package you sent and will take everything on our trip. So for today we send love, keep the letters coming and we'll do the same.

Your loving Daddy

That time in my memory ...

The respites of summer in the country always seemed to have a reviving effect. In retrospect, I am now so grateful that many of our relatives lived "on the land" and not in the cities. At times I had wished their lives were more sophisticated and citified, but looking back, it was a life-saving existence. The social aspects of "having each other" can never be overstated.

I was almost glad to get home from camp, as I had another fall from the horse and had to drop out of all riding activities. Some of my friends had left with the rumor that a case of polio had been discovered. That of course was the most dreaded disease of the times—afflicting even President Roosevelt.

My mind was already focused on beginning high school, and the prospect of going school shopping filled me with great joy. Going to high school was to be more complex than grammar school. It would involve train rides and all their schedules or being driven by Arnold. I was not so much in favor of the latter, as it would be awkward to explain to my schoolmates why I came in a chauffer-driven car, but these were minor details that would easily be ironed out.

As I mentioned before, the prospect of going to New Trier and ultimately, Northwestern was exhilarating. It was the pattern for so many of my schoolmates on the North Shore—a foregone conclusion.

August 17, 1936

Dear daughter Thea,

You will be surprised to hear how much we enjoy our summer in the country in Schwegenheim. We could not ask for more if we were tourists from a foreign land. Of course, much of the enjoyment is being with the relatives, working along beside them to bring in the harvest. The only disappointment was the cherries. The rainy cold summer is responsible for that. However, we're looking forward to a great picking holiday. I have even learned to split wood, which the relatives are stacking up for winter. Many greetings to you from people you may not even remember, but they all remember you. One young man brought Mother some lovely flowers, a bouquet of daisies in your honor. He said that you used to tease him a lot about his red hair and that he did not know enough poetry.

I am sure when you're back from camp you will contact the aunts and uncles in Chicago again. By the way, thank you for explaining what a musical is. "Play with music" sounds very logical; that you are all writing it yourselves sounds very impressive. That the star is a young lady who will be going to Hollywood is also very interesting. Is she the same young lady who starred in last year's production? It sounds like you have a bigger role in this one. You must let us know how it all comes out when you present it on parents' weekend. It sounds like the making of a film itself.

I am falling behind in my English, but will resume it when I get back home. I hope we will be asked to Stuttgart again very soon. That is always an incentive to continue my English studies.

For today a tired, aching, but happy Pappa and family greet you.

That time in my memory ...

I was constantly amazed how Pappa took to working in the fields: He certainly never had that background growing up! Philosophical, and intellectually inclined, he admired the hard labors of others, but had never been called upon to do it himself.

An interesting comment was about the redheaded young man who brought mother some flowers. As I remembered, I did tease him about not knowing enough poetry. He was ambitious for all the good things in life. I wonder if he ever achieved them under Hitler.

Returning from camp, I was caught up in still settling into the new house with all activities centering on school. The first week Arnold was to drive me and pick me up, but then I was to have a "tripper" ticket on the North Shore Line like all the other students. I couldn't wait! It would make it easier and more fun to ride with my classmates. The prospect of being in that large a school had me worrying—will I be lost in the crowd or still have the individual attention of the teachers? Other anxieties were concerning, would I be ready for a certain class? There was still so much of English I had to learn. Math would be no problem.

Meanwhile, Aunt Anne tried to distract me with back-to-school shopping, trips and weekend activities involving my friends and the Perlstein relatives.

23

September 1936

HEADLINES OF THE DAY:

ROME—Italy Sends Warships to Spain after Murder of Italian Citizen

BERLIN—Reich Orders Confiscation of 25% of Jewish Fortunes

PARIS—France Signs Treaties with Syria and Lebanon, Promising Independence in Three Years

NUREMBERG—Hitler Denies War Aims, Asserts Right to Colonies

GENEVA—Italy Asks League of Nations to Bar Ethiopian Delegates

UNITED STATES—Father Coughlin, Right Wing Priest, Rebuked by Vatican for Anti-Semitic Remarks

September 6, 1936

My dear Thea,

Although there was no letter from you this week I don't want to wait any longer to wish you a blessed Rosh Hashanah—a blessed New Year. I hope that in the coming year you will again be blessed with the good luck, the good health that has followed you all your young life.

No doubt, with a wonderful vacation behind you, you started a new phase of your education, in high school. You have been rather vague as to where you are going. Both of the schools you mentioned sound excellent, so do let us know which one you finally choose. It sounds like you have to travel a while on the train or by car for either one of them, but the main thing is the education you receive there.

Although we have been getting some fall weather, full of chilly rains, today is a beautiful day—the kind you used to love for the *Kirchmess (fall carnival)*. There are no politics there, just great fun, and Ruth is taking full advantage of it. I remember you coming home, smelling of roasted almonds and telling us all about the fate of the Titanic, the predictions of Nostradamus, and how the Chinese would rule the world in the year 3000. The Gypsy predictions seem to have come true—you're in another world, another life.

The Benkers [*old friends of Pappa's*] returned from America and have built a beautiful house here. Since he will have an official post in the government, it is only fitting that they live well. They are decent people who still remember that we helped them in their bad times and have invited us for coffee. Mamma is hesitant about going, but I will convince her for old time's sake, she should go. I hate seeing her become so uncertain and afraid. She will not go anywhere but to the relatives on our trips.

I hope your next letter will bring the answers to all my many questions. They are only the longings of an anxious father. With the triple blessing upon you, I remain your affectionate father.

Your Daddy

That time in my memory …

Another Rosh Hashanah, the New Year looms without knowing what it will bring. I am anxious to start high school at one of the finest high schools in the country; New Trier High School in Winnetka. The other schools we were considering were a country day school and a young ladies' seminary, both private and conservative. As I mentioned before, I liked the idea of a big public school, New Trier.

I was really concerned about the change in Mamma, from someone as outgoing as she was, to become almost a recluse. Still she was buoyed by Pappa's enthusiasm, and that meant everything to me. As I recall, I went to spend the holidays with my relatives and went to services with them as I had promised. The Perlstein family celebrated with Aunt Anne's father, Grandpa Agazim, and all that side of the family. Quite a large gathering as she had 3 brothers and a sister, all living in the Chicago-Milwaukee area. I really wanted to be with them. However, there was a warm welcome from my aunt and her extensive family in Chicago. They were something new in my relationship—the non-observant American Jew, who only remembered the rituals at Rosh Hashanah and Yom Kippur. Most of them never learned to speak German and had become totally assimilated in life in America. Their professions were in pharmaceutical distribution; one was a lawyer and another owned a furniture store. Their interests were in sports and in politics, with no great concern for their European relatives and their fate.

Letter from Gerda:

September 20, 1936

Dear Little Thea,

I know I said I would not call you little again, but it does slip out, so I will try to remember that you are growing into a young lady. I don't want to be considered an old-fashioned sister by your friends when you read them my letters. Thank you so much for your explicit letters, I feel much more your contemporary than your older sister. Camp really sounds wonderful; so many activities that let your mind and imagination grow. Don't feel guilty that you have all this while Ruth has so little. She too will have it someday, and you can show her how to enjoy it.

Becoming a young woman can be very trying. You are subject to moods and feelings you can't quite understand at times. Just remember that I am here when you need to talk. Keep a diary; it can hold your innermost thoughts, intimate secrets, and longings. I wish I were with you in the States, to be closer when you need me, but that seems farther away than ever.

The Olympic Games are over, but many Americans are still in town. Of course the big attraction was Jesse Owens who disproved all of Mr. Hitler's theories, a magnificent man of dignity and courage.

I go to the port and watch the great ships sail away, ships like the 'Europa', 'Bremen', and 'Columbus.' I wish I were on them. I am switching back to English, which I am trying to recall more and more. I read a lot of English books lately, also some good American authors, who are very real or realistic, which is correct? I take a small sailboat out to sea. The little ship *schaukelt*[1] (I don't know the English word for that), but I am not "sea-ill". Now that your high school has begun, how do you like it? How does it compare to the school you have just left? I know it is not like our *Lyceum* or *Gymnasium (German secondary schools)*. I better switch to German again; the questions are easier to form.

I hope all the subjects you are taking will prepare you for a future at the university, it is an exciting prospect. My dear doctor is away again, so I am all alone in the big house. Write again and use all the paper. Remember, it will cost the same to fill both sides. Please let me know what fills your days and your thoughts. It makes me feel like I'm in that other world with you.

Your loving sister—Gerda

---

1.   Sways or rocks

That time in my memory ...

Gerda is once again full of advice and I took her up on her suggestion to keep a diary. I wonder why I hadn't thought of it before. It does make some of my feelings easier to live with and, possibly, understand. There were still a lot of questions on my mind—some I really felt too hesitant to take to Aunt Anne, but then I probably wouldn't have taken them to my mother either. The diary was a wonderful idea. Over the years it became a repository for poems and sketches. I wish I still had it, but over the years it seems to have disappeared. I started one again when I went to Japan, but that too is gone. What has survived is a book of poems in lavender ink, and faded thoughts of the world around me, the tragedy in human lives but the survival of the spirit.

School had begun and I must say I felt right at home. Not only were there familiar faces from camp and Fortnightly, but the teachers were personal and warm. And thank heaven I did make the experimental classes, though I wasn't quite sure what the difference would be from the regular ones. I also had my first classmate luncheon at Cooley's Cupboard in Evanston, something that was to become a tradition.

September 30, 1936

Dear daughter Thea,

We received your letter from the 16th of September, and since we haven't written in a while, I will reply to it immediately. I might say the same goes for those from Elsie and Gerda. As I always tell you, regarding our health we have no complaints. Our holidays were solemn and quiet in reverence and atonement, with fervent wishes for a better future. You did not mention how you spent yours. Were you able to leave school and attend services? High school must be even more difficult than our secondary schools, with many more subjects than we have here right now. I don't know what all is being taught except a new, revised version of Germany and world history and religion. Ruth is still allowed at school, but we have no idea how much longer, so we must prepare to instruct her at home.

The town life goes on with birth, death, and tragedies. There are daily incidents of what I consider man's inhumanity to his fellow man. No matter how hard Herr Hitler tries, he cannot change that in human nature; rather, right now, he helps it along in all its bestiality.

Our friends, the Benkers, from America, are settled in their new home. Mamma and Ruth have been invited over, and nobody dares tell the Benkers that it isn't the thing to do anymore. The town is still sprucing up, with newly plastered houses and newly paved streets and sidewalks. They are much easier to march on with heavy boots than the clay streets we had before. Winter is already making itself felt. This morning the roofs were white with frost, and we needed extra wood on the fire. Yesterday we gathered the last of the plums, and Mamma will make a big batch of plum butter for the relatives, another hedge against winter. We'll be traveling again to help with the potato and apple harvest. We are drawn more and more to the land and all it provides. How different from how you spend your days!

You take the train to school, go to classes all day, then meet with the friends and teachers to discuss the day or participate in sports. Then the train home, chats and dinner with the family and homework, homework. It is a very good program for the future. Hearing all of that, Ruth no longer complains about all the she has to do at school. Write again soon and receive all our love.

Your Daddy

That time in my memory ...

Pappa writes of the Benker family returning to Germany. Mr. Benker became a high town official, but never forgot his debt to my father. The Benkers were always ready with hospitality to my family, and no one in town challenged them about it.

Helping with the fall harvest was another respite for the family, as well as a provider for the winter ahead. At least they had the opportunity to return to the land. Many city Jews did not have that option. Some of the debts were paid with the barter system—food for past debts to the store. It worked out very well.

For me, it was like living in two worlds. The uneasy what-will-happen-tomorrow that Pappa writes about, and the fairy land that was my present home. The uneasiness in Europe concerning Franco's successes in Spain was the big concern. Pappa seemed to feel that it would not alter their situation very much, although Hitler and Franco were men of the same fascist beliefs.

Here, high school was an entirely different experience. Since we still lived in Highland Park, I had to take the train to school early in the morning. That made for a very long day. As I have mentioned before, New Trier was a unique experience in education. I no longer had the fear of being left behind. On the contrary, with experimental classes, and exposure to the arts by W.P.A. artists and performers, it was opening another world.

Someone once said: "You never forget your hardest, most demanding teachers." In my case, it was my English teacher, Miss Vlasto. There was no catering to my language shortcoming—Miss Vlasto was a stern taskmaster. Today I look upon her as sort of a kin of Shaw's Henry Higgins in drilling me on proper English and how to get rid of my guttural "R's". Unlike today's immigrant children, who are taught in their own language, it made the integration into the American System that much easier. The pride in one's heritage should not be forgotten, but fitting into mainstream America is equally important—it was to me.

24

October 1936

HEADLINES OF THE DAY:

VIENNA—Chancellor Schusschnigg Dissolves Fascist Bodies, Becomes Dictator

GREAT BRITAIN—British Fascist Oswald Mosley Leads Anti-Semitic March in London

GERMANY—Germany Sends "Condor Legion" Military Unit to Fight with Nationalist Rebels in Spain

BERLIN—Hitler and Ciano, Italian Foreign Minister Draft Treaty of Alliance

ALBANY, NY—Alfred Smith Accuses FDR of Paving Way for Communism with his Social Programs

October 21, 1936

Dear little daughter,

We are already in October and as kitchen chef, housemaid, and teacher, my time is well taken up. I am not the chef, as you are, being taught by your Irish cook, but I feed Ruth and myself very well while Mamma is away. She is enjoying herself so much, we told her to stay with her sister as long as she likes. Max took her to a concert in Speyer, and it was like old times, when she used to go to concerts regularly.

Your cooking lessons sound quite different from mine. I'm not sure how "Grapefruit a la the Prince of Wales" fits into our potato and herring menu, but I will not worry about it since we have never had grapefruit and probably never will.

Although the relatives write they have not seen you since the holidays, I'm glad you took the time to visit them and go to synagogue. We are awaiting a visit from Gerda. It will be good to see her and have some frank face-to-face talks. It is most difficult for her to adjust to a life without her husband and the future they had planned together, but she is a woman of spirit and determination.

Give me more information about your new school. The fact that it is called New Trier, since the town where I came from is Old Trier, is most interesting. Do you know who the benefactors were who founded the school? It interests me to know who they were. Do you still have the little silver replica of the "Porta Negra", the Trier landmark I gave you a long time ago? If you still do, show it to your teacher and principal and tell them the background of the landmark. Ruth wants to write a few words, so I close now with affectionate kisses.

Your Daddy

Dear Sister,

See how my handwriting has improved. Pappa and I are doing fine even without Mamma. Now that I can have a cot in their room I can sleep much better. I can't wait for your next package—I know it will be good. They still have wool in the sock shops, so I will make you something warm.

Meanwhile, I'm still allowed at school, as Herr Steuer and some of the others stick up for me. Even Fraulein Wiedeman, who is a real Nazi, and worships Hitler, is in my corner. How is that for a surprise? She was a Nazi even while you were here. She keeps an autographed picture of Hitler in a silver frame on her desk and kisses it.

Pappa is making potato pancakes and applesauce for dinner, so I have to help.

Goodbye now and be good—

Love and kisses.—Ruth

That time in my memory ...

At this time, the family menus at home were very simple. Meat was scarce, except for horsemeat, which they didn't eat. Chicken was still available, but most of their meals were built around preserved fruit with whole-wheat dumplings, potato and herring salad, or a baked fish, which Daddy continued to catch.

Here, of course, it was something else. Mealtimes were quite a ritual in the Perlstein household as so often there were guests. At the time, I wasn't very impressed by names like Morgenthau and Baruch, but the show business people always left me in a state of awe. We were always "dressed" at dinnertime and on our best behavior. I was always delighted to answer the many questions about Germany, but didn't feel there was a great concern about an ominous future for the Jews, except by Mr. Morgenthau and Mr. Baruch.

To prepare "Grapefruit a la Prince of Wales (later the Duke of Windsor)" was quite a culinary achievement. I learned it from the new butler, who was a former employee of the Prince. It required the delicate removal of the membrane, leaving the fruit intact, and topping it with a cherry or strawberry. In the winter it was broiled with brown sugar and bread crumbs.

Mr. Ashton, the new butler, was a middle-aged gentleman who wore striped trousers and a double breasted jacket on the job. The severity of this outfit was mitigated by a gaily-colored breast pocket handkerchief, which was of a different pattern everyday. He reminded me a lot of Anthony Eden without the mustache. Mr. Ashton came to us just before the Prince of Wales became Edward VIII and later the Duke of Windsor. I suppose it was a long, not-so-nice story. Today, it would probably bring him a lot of money blabbing about the royals to the tabloids. All I remember is he was kind, recognizing me as a fellow European. For my birthday he gave me a jar of Bar Le Duc jelly (white currants) from which he made tiny sandwiches to accompany the Cambric tea he made me when I came home from school. Now and then, he spoke of Edward, Prince of Wales, and "that woman", who of course was to become the Duchess of Windsor. Although I had a very good rapport with him, the gentleman didn't last very long in our household. His superior attitude as a former royal employee made it difficult for the other servants to accept him. They took a petition to Aunt Anne stating their discontent with the 'gentleman.' She, of course, complied with their vote and in truly democratic fashion gave him his notice in the interest of harmony in the household. I really missed him. He had such jolly stories to tell me about England and his former employers.

I became more and more fascinated with the story of my high school, New Trier, since Pappa came from Old Trier on the Moselle. Apparently, education was provided by a settler named Franz Joseph Hoffman, a son of an "Old Trier" settler as early as 1846. School houses were built in Winnetka as early as 1859 and Glencoe in 1856.

Those who wanted to continue their education went to Evanston or even as far as Chicago. One of the first to inspire the building of a high school for the growing villages of the North Shore was General Charles H. Howard, who in May 1899 became the first head of the Board of Education. In August, the taxpayers authorized $60,000 to purchase a tract of land in Winnetka and erect a large tower building. The name of course was derived from the early settlers. New Trier opened in 1901 with seventy six students and seven teachers. Its growth was phenomenal and by 1929, it had courses that did not exist in other high schools. It also had an advisory system which placed 30 students under the guidance of one advisor. By the time I arrived, experimental classes were in full swing, and exchange teachers from abroad were also part of the faculty. There were also enhancing programs by W.P.A. artists. To make the arts part of the school curriculum was absolutely revolutionary and to me one of the most positive programs that was initiated under FDR. It not only employed the hundreds of artists who had no public exposure, but it nurtured thousands of students in the pleasures of the arts.

25

November 1936

HEADLINES OF THE DAY:

UNITED STATES—Roosevelt Elected to Second Term in White House

ITALY—Mussolini Announces Pact with Hitler; Urges France & Britain to Join

WASHINGTON—Government Reports Highest Level of Business Since 1930

SPAIN—Rome and Berlin Recognize Franco Government in Burgos

BERLIN—Nazis Drop 1000s of "Alien" Words from German Language; Users Threatened with Fine or Imprisonment

NEW YORK—100,000 Watch Navy Beats Army 7-0 in Final Three Minutes

November 15, 1936

Dear Thea,

We don't want to wait any longer for your letter to arrive, since we have been without one for about three weeks. We hope it is not due to some unusual happening, rather the irregular quirks of the weather and the mails. Hopefully there's always tomorrow. Gerda has been gone again for a week, and the place is quiet as before. Mamma, in spite of the hard work bringing in the harvest with the relatives, had a wonderful time taking in concerts and theater. It is remarkable how she can switch from one role to the other. During her absence my cooking did improve, though I didn't get into tortes and cakes. Most of those require an abundance of butter, eggs, sugar and chocolate, and those ingredients are almost impossible for us to buy. Besides, trying to read your grandmother's spidery, albeit beautiful, handwritten recipes are difficult indeed.

We again hope you are in good health, in spite of our frugal meals, we can report the same. So happy to hear that you received another wonderful winter wardrobe. Don't forget to send Ruth all you cannot wear, as we no longer carry any ready-made clothing in the store (or what is left of it). Since Mamma was lucky enough to find someone to sew for her at night, she unearthed some rough hand-woven cloth that no one wanted and is making coats out of it. Almost everything is knitted by her and Lenchen. Please let us know when you send a package, so we can alert the post office.

The relatives from Landstuhl will visit you at the end of February. They were just here to purchase their tickets for a visit over there. These are easy to get, if you have the money and are not leaving permanently. Emigration is another story. Gretel has made very good connections with a public official and is thinking of getting married: Why not? She is a beautiful girl.

I hope your teacher will contact us when she gets here. It would really be quite an event all around. She will be able to give you a first hand report of all that is going on with us.

We haven't really resumed our English lessons, rather we wait until we hear that we are actually going. Hopefully there is a letter in the mail.

Until then—Your devoted Pappa

That time in my memory ...

I could never understand why the relatives from Landstuhl would only want to visit the U.S. and not stay there. Now I realize that they could only get temporary visas to visit Gretel, who was getting married.

One of my teachers from New Trier was visiting Germany and promised to visit my parents. It was all very exciting for me as well as to them. She had promised to take some much needed food packages with her but we didn't want her to get into trouble so Pappa said to limit them to sugar, tea, and chocolate; things she might like to have on the trip herself. She would also take books for Ruth, as English books were no longer available in the German book stores. This link between my past and present was very important to me: It gave me a sense of reality in a still hard-to-imagine world that alternated between sunlight and shadow.

November 29, 1936

Dearest Thea,

Your letter written on the train to school arrived right after our last one left here. It was good luck, as a whole raft of others arrived at the same time. I am still trying to find a system that would speed up the mail back and forth, perhaps by writing so the letters are shipped on "The United States" line. See, now I am even becoming a transportation expert.

Our health, thanks to G-d, leaves nothing to complain about. It seems odd that in the midst of all our trials and stress, our mental and physical being remains on even keel. I suppose our hope in you and our eventual reunion is accountable for that. Strangely enough, this winter, there are more German suicides than I have heretofore encountered. Gerda, in her studies of psychiatry, has made us more aware of that.

You must know how we appreciated the visit of Ms. Karsh, and that she bore such a good message from you. That, plus the pictures and gifts, made it most memorable. Your parents' evening in school sounded most interesting, especially the difference between her impression and those you have from your childhood. The fact that your school is named New Trier, after my own birthplace, made it an interesting link to the past. I'm still hoping you can find out the name of the family who established it.

We had news from Wawern. Uncle Benny also bought a farm in Luxembourg where his family will practice agriculture. They all went there except Jennie, who is determined to go to Palestine. It will be quite a change for the boys from their studies of law and philosophy. One by one, they leave Germany. Soon we, the older generation, shall be the only ones left. We shall probably go to say our goodbyes to them around Christmas time.

Continue to enjoy all the gifts offered to you. For you the weeks seem to fly by. Ruth is sending you a poem she wrote about the joy of Chanukah.

It is just two years since you left, and all the changes we have both seen, yours for the better, thank G-d. We're having our first snow; may it be a mild winter.

With ever-giving love—Your Dad

That time in my memory …

Again "Pappa's" ("Dad's") reassurance that they were physically well eased some of my concerns. Mrs. Karsh's good report of her visit with them made it even easier to be optimistic.

She and I became much closer when she returned with a first hand report of my parents' circumstances. I continued the life of a privileged youngster. With every positive advantage offered to me, I tried even harder to please everyone. Sometimes it felt like a heavy burden that I had to carry. I felt like I was living two lives at once.

I loved school, every subject was approached in a novel way; in music we had to set the mood for the music we were hearing; in English, we wrote headlines à la the Tribune. My only complaint, were the blue frozen knees I had when we played hockey early on those cold November mornings.

Meanwhile, I had written Pappa the history of New Trier and again thought it kind of an omen that linked me with Pappa's past.

A word about Uncle Benny: He had an interesting odyssey: From Luxembourg, he went to Bolivia, and after the War resettled in Luxembourg, never being without his precious Torah. It was still enshrined in his living room when I visited him many years later. One of his sons settled in the United States, and the other became a noted politician in Luxembourg after the War.

26

December 1936

HEADLINES OF THE DAY:

GREAT BRITAIN—King Edward VIII Abdicates Throne to Marry American Divorcee

BUENOS AIRES—FDR Opens Pan-American Conference

SPAIN—Rebels Bomb Catalonia for the First Time

INDIA—Nehru Urges India to Strike at British Imperialism

GERMANY—Nazi Exhibit of "Degenerate Art" Draws Largest Public Gathering of any Art Show in Germany

December 9, 1936

My Dear Child,

Unfortunately, the wish for a mild winter is not being granted, but at least it satisfies Ruth's love of the winter sports. We are cozy and snug by the fire, and the harvest Mamma helped bring in keeps us fed and in good health.

The newspapers continue to be full of rules and new laws, not just for us, but for the party members themselves. Now they are codified as The Nuremberg Laws and are even more harsh and restricting. It is as if every adult were the child of the state, incapable of forming his own thoughts.

Although there is much to do about Christmas and the lighting of a huge tree in every town in Germany, there is no intimate family joy as there used to be.

You mentioned of going to a camp reunion with your campmates in Chicago. That should be a nice holiday event for you. If you do not go with the family to Arizona, where will you stay? I am sure Aunt Anne has it all worked out, so I will not worry about it.

For today we send all our love, Your Pappa and Devoted Family.

As always, your Dad

P.S. Ruth is very excited about the package you will send. I hope it gets here. Many packages, especially those going to the cities, seem never to arrive. Thank G-d our postal workers are honest. The new postman, just as our old one, keeps us well ahead of the delivery list, and we are most grateful for that.

That time in my memory ...

As Pappa writes, they had been fortunate with the postman, the old one as well as the new. They announced my letter deliveries ahead of time, brought packages without opening them, and stamped Dad's letters officially without censoring them (all letters in Germany were subject to official censorship, and could not be delivered without the regime's "approval" of the contents).

I did not go to Arizona with the family, as I wanted to be in town for my camp reunion. These contacts were very important to me. I stayed with Grandpa Agazim, Aunt Anne's father in Chicago. Grandpa Agazim had been born in Russia and had a large apartment in Chicago. He was a delightful old gentleman with a crown of snow white hair. That, and his leathery tan skin, had me fascinated every time I saw him. He seemed ageless to me. There was constantly a lighted cigarette between his fingers.

He taught me the rudiments of chess and reminisced about the "old country" and the pogroms of persecution. To him, Hitler was nothing new. To my delight, his house-keeper had a grandson a few years older than I was. He took me to the movies and ice skating, which made the holidays busy and pleasant. Then, too, there was Aunt Min Lesser, Aunt Anne's sister, to keep an eye on me and take me shopping. I loved going to the Jewish delicatessen on Argyle Street with her. Jewish delicatessens are totally differ-ent from German ones. The sounds, the sights, and the smells all blend into something much more exotic. Smoked fish mingled with onion bialys, and how could those poi-sonous looking pickles in the barrel taste so good? I wanted to make a nut torte, so I asked the counterman for a pound of tonsils. "What?" he exclaimed, in a shocked voice. Aunt Min also looked up in surprise. "You know, this kind of nut" and I held up a nut still in its shell from an open bag. "Oh, you mean almonds," he laughed, obviously relieved. So once again, I learned a lesson as before: Certain words can have a double meaning. The German word "Mandeln" can be translated as either almonds or tonsils, depending on how you intend to use it.

The camp reunion was everything it could have been at Marshall Fields and the Palmer House. It ended with lots of invitations to visit all around, and great opti-mism for next summer's camp session.

Europe and its problems again seemed so very far away ...

December 18, 1936

My dearest Thea,

Christmas is almost upon us, and Chanukah passed quietly without any great exchange of gifts, only the necessities, like warm boots, caps, and mittens. We had our traditional pancakes and candle lighting. Our good neighbors did remember us with simple gifts, like a homemade cake or a dozen eggs. A total surprise was a bottle of *Asbach Uralt* for my birthday: this was rare indeed, as many "state endorsed" people cannot even get it. I am grateful of the many anonymous donors who thought of me so warmly; may G-d bless them all!

Mamma and Ruth are knitting scarves and caps for all those we know and care about. They even want to send a set to you, although I assured them that those have surely been provided for you.

We were glad to hear you are staying with friends as well as "Grandpa Agazim." All those downtown outings and concerts must have given you special pleasure and memories. What is "Christmas at Field's?" You mentioned a big department store with beautiful decorations and entertainment as a place where all your camp-mates came together.

Dear child—that is what the magic of the holidays should be all about; Chanukah with its miracle and for our Christian friends their miracle of birth; treasure them. Write soon, and go to see the relatives when you are able: you must know it keeps peace in the family.

Your loving Father, Mamma, and Ruth

That time in my memory ...

The gift of Asbach Uralt, Dad's favorite brandy, by anonymous friends was an overwhelming surprise to everyone. To know that he still had standing in the community was a heart-warming tribute.

Somehow, in spite of their being ostracized, they still had warm and loyal friends, maybe not as many as before, but sincere and caring. It could not have been easy for their friends either

As for the celebration with my camp-mates, it was traditionally advertised: "Christmas isn't Christmas without a day at Fields." During holiday time, the famous department store downtown, Chicago, was decorated from basement through its nine stories of merchandise. It boasted the tallest Christmas tree this side of the White House, with oversized decorations and trimmings. Years later, when working for the art department, I remember designing some of those outsized ornaments. The upper story of the huge store was devoted to the "Cloud Cottage" a fantasy house where Mr., and Mrs. Mistletoe reigned over all the gifts that a heart could desire, strategically placed throughout the cottage, of course. Luncheon at Fields was as always a traditional festive affair with Fields' Special (an open-faced sandwich) and Frango mints (their world famous chocolates) in every form imaginable. All this accompanied by the famed Chicago Opera Chorus or church choirs from the area—it was a treat for eyes and ears.

So while Mamma and Ruth were knitting much-needed scarves and mittens, I was faced with a myriad display of all sorts of unbelievable luxuries. Our camp luncheon, with a preview of the new camp uniforms, was a wonderful taste of things to come.

I didn't miss going to Arizona at all!

December 30, 1936

My Dear Child,

Ahead of us is the New Year: 1937. What will it bring for all of us? Although the snows of Christmas are beautiful, it is very cold, and they keep everyone indoors. Of course for us this is not unusual, as Mamma will not leave the house. With Ruth, it is more difficult; but she writes her poetry, reads, and beats us all at cards.

Your holidays sounded so beautiful, even without going to Arizona. You have been doing many interesting things; the music class for children, for instance. Dr. Stock (Frederick Stock, who conducted the Chicago Symphony Orchestra until 1942) sounds like a wonderful man, and that he reminds you of grandfather is quite a tribute to the latter. The fact that you spoke German to him makes him even more familiar and endearing. We envy you the live music, but we do have our phonograph and radio. At least the Christmas music is a change from the eternal marches and songs to German glory.

We have been to Wawern to say goodbye. Hopefully we can see them again in the future. When, only G-d knows. Uncle Benny is taking the Ark and Torah with him, and that is a comfort. To return to the land will be quite a change for them. The boys say that it will be the age of the educated farmer. A story is passing around about two highly respected rabbis who were pulling a dung wagon and discussing the philosophies of Kierkegaard and Buber. Anything is possible within the spirit; you must remember that, as you continue your education.

Your reunion with your campmates sounded very nostalgic. The fact that your camp parents had all of your bunkmates (what is "bunk?") overnight sounds very brave. I can imagine a houseful of chattering and giggling young ladies all night long. I am sure that no one slept.

Ruth says she would like to send you her poetry, so you can read it to your many friends, and she will be famous before you. Mamma is very grateful for the theater programs and the news of Richard Tauber in England. The silk shawl you sent her is beautiful, and she wears it every night.

We bless you, dear child, as we hope the New Year brings us all closer to each other.

With much love from all, Your Dad

That time in my memory ...

I had chosen not to accompany my foster family to Arizona, but to remain in Chicago for Dr. Stock's Symphony Party for Children, Christmas at Marshall Field's, and, of course, my camp-mates' reunion, all as described in previous letters

New Years was spent with my friend, Alice Ruth Berlin, whose father although named Irving, was not the famous songwriter. We went to our Fortnightly New Years Dance, which was the crowning conclusion to our Christmas holidays. A nephew of Uncle Harry's was my escort in proper evening clothes with an equally proper corsage. It sounds romantic, but he was much older than I, and would rather have spent the evening with one of the Chez Paree showgirls, which was his usual social life. Escorting me must have been a sacrifice.

Nevertheless, he was very attentive and made me feel very grown up. I did look very grown up with a peach gown embroidered with coral beads from Martha Weathered Shop at the Drake Hotel. That was the height of elegance. That, and my older escort made the other girls more curious and added to the spice of the evening.

Meanwhile, preparations were being made for the re-opening of school. We were notified that we would be getting exchange teachers from England in some of our subjects, and I was to have a teacher from Cardiff as my math instructor.

I looked forward to the family coming back. Even though the house was fully staffed, when I came back from Grandpa Agazim's, I was lonely. I didn't realize how much I missed the children.

27

January 1937

HEADLINES OF THE DAY:

UNITED STATES—In Inaugural Speech, FDR Pledges to Aid Under-Privileged

PALESTINE—Jerusalem Mufti Tells British Jewish Immigration Must Cease

WASHINGTON—Government Bars Americans from Serving in Spanish War

MEXICO—Trotsky Arrives in Mexico; Condemned in Absentia by Stalin

GERMANY—Hitler Guarantees Neutrality of Belgium and Holland

UNITED STATES—Mellon Donates $19 Million in Art to the People of the U.S.

January 14, 1937

Dear Daughter Thea,

My, you are growing into a young lady indeed! The photo of the New Year's dance is beautiful, and so are you in the evening gown. The young man with whom you are dancing: Is he from your school? You do not write much about boys in your life, but knowing you, you must have some good friends among them. The gentleman who escorted you, the cousin of Uncle Harry's, must have made you feel very grown up, indeed. We thank him for substituting for your foster parent at this event. It is very flattering that he brought you a corsage, and that you are preserving it as a memento of a lovely evening is a very grown-up, romantic thing to do. Store all your good memories, as we do, and bury the others. Right now you cannot see it, but a rich life contains both the bitter and the sweet.

We are still in the grip of a deadly winter, and many friends have passed away. The earth is frozen too solid to bury them, so they are kept in the church, where we go to pay our last respects. Ruth has not started back to school. It has been closed because of the bad weather and so many ailing children.

You must be back at your studies by now. I'm not really surprised that you like the painting and music courses best, but remember English, Math, French, and History broaden the base for earning your future living.

You describe a new sport in which you are participating, Lacrosse. I have never heard of it, but then, as much as I know of the Old World, I know so little about the New, especially about the American Indian culture, where you say this sport has its origin. Although the cowboy stories call them savages, they have an ancient culture we must never belittle. Look at all the crafts you made in camp: they all originated from the Indians.

So your foster family is back home again and you are all looking forward to many new adventures in the coming year. I know you will keep us posted on all of them.

We all send our love, Your Devoted Father

That time in my memory ...

As mentioned in another letter, here was the other reason I didn't want to go to Arizona: the dancing school had planned a grown-up New Year's Ball with all the courtesies and celebrations of dinner, dancing, and the welcoming of the New Year.

*The boys at Fortnightly, for the most part, were very immature with few excep-
tions. I felt years older. Here again, what we called the "WASP" tradition prevailed,
and most of them couldn't have been less interested in the little "foreigner". Here, too,
I found out the difference between "old money' and "new money", and that I would
never be eligible for the Junior League.*

*The old admonition: "Keep the Arts as an avocation" still dominated Pappa's
advice. The road to making a respectable living was still through the Academic studies
of English, Math, Languages and History.*

*Lacrosse was a new sport on my spring activity list, and l looked eagerly forward to
it. Many of the girls preferred it as a team sport, as it made for closer cooperation and
sportsmanship. We also were to pick "Pen Pals" through our French class, and correspond with a student in France. Learning the formal French Language was quite different from the French/German patois that Grandfather spoke. It was interesting,
finally to recognize which words were German and which were French: That was
something I had not been aware of before. Knowing the French words gave me a head
start in the program, and brought memories of my grandfather very much to mind.*

January 26, 1937

My Dear Daughter,

Other than through the mail, we feel cut off from the world. It doesn't look as though spring will ever come. Ruth took the letter to your old teachers at school, and they were delighted to hear from you. Your friend Elfriede has made you a needle case and has asked Ruth to send it on to you, since she dare not mail it herself.

The New Year has brought many more restrictions and laws. The Jews are much worse off in the cities, where some still had good businesses. Some had been there for centuries and still had them confiscated as "illegally acquired." It is incredible how they can justify such a thing to the public! I will be going on another trip, hopefully not too long, but Mamma and Ruth cannot go with me, but they will be all right, and take care of each other.

It sounds as though you are busier than ever, with a new activity at the Art Institute of Chicago, a painting class. We congratulate you on winning a "Junior Scholarship" and thank your teachers who proposed you. Will you still have time for your music classes with Dr. Stock?

The pictures of the new house are beautiful. Once spring comes, the outside will be as beautiful as the inside. Remember that nothing can improve on nature, but the beautiful house seems to fit right in with the lovely scenery.

We are translating the little article from the school paper, which mentions your ancestors as being from "Old Trier", and that you are now a student at "New Trier." Everything will come full cycle; such is human nature. That is why I think this, too, shall pass. They speak of "a Thousand Year Reich." I venture to say that in a hundred years, it will only have been a ripple in history. People in the world are too wise to let outrages go on forever and let humanity perish.

We are hopeful we will have another bid for the consulate soon. Meanwhile we send our love and wait for your next adventure.

Your Devoted Dad:

That time in my memory ...

As Dad had written in January 1935, people were already beginning to see just how restrictive the Nazi regime intended to be. In this letter he gave me the opportunity to see the ever-growing web of restrictions and laws that entangled the German Jews. Jews from other European countries no doubt looked on in quiet horror, thankful only that these constraints were no part of their lives. Between 1939 and 1942, they were to learn first-hand the terrors that Nazism held for Jews of any nation.

As for our family, Dad was again hopefully awaiting a bid from the American Consulate in Stuttgart, an invitation that would put him, Mamma, and Ruth beyond the reach of such horrors and despicable inhumanity.

As we know now, that agency at the time was not very sympathetic to Jewish refugees; no matter what President Roosevelt's politics proclaimed. Most of their sympathies were with the efficiency of the "New Order."

Pappa still did not want me to approach the Perlsteins for an affidavit; he still wanted to do it through his own channels, the help of the relatives and business friends. I complied, even though I wanted to find a way to allay their disappointment with the "official channels."

The "Junior Scholarship" at the Art Institute came through a nomination by my art teachers at New Trier High School, Mr. and Mrs. Frank Holland. It meant a class of instructions every Saturday. My delight at this development had no bounds. This was the career I wanted, something having to do with the "Creative Arts." I could spend all of Saturday in town, in the morning at the Art Institute, and in the afternoon with the Symphony's children's program: A full day with the arts. I dropped Ballet, as I was getting too" fleshy" to be a ballerina. Aunt Anne said the money was not wasted, as it gave me an appreciation of how hard a ballerina had to work to achieve excellence; it also taught me how to enter a room without falling flat on my face.

28

February 1937

HEADLINES OF THE DAY:

MICHIGAN—Troops Surround GM Plants Following Strike Riots

MOSCOW—Russia Executes 13 Trotskyites

UNITED STATES—DuPont Patents Nylon—Revolutionary New Thread

PARIS—House of Deputies Vote 19 Billion Francs for Defense to Match German Reich Budget for Military Build-Up

ETHIOPIA—Italians Annihilate 3,000 Rebels Planning Attack on Addis Ababa

SAN FRANCISCO—Ten Workers Die as Scaffolding Collapses on Golden Gate Bridge

February 3, 1937

Dear Little Thea

Though our replies to your last two letters may have been long in coming, please forgive us as we all have been suffering from attacks of the *Grippe* (influenza). Thankfully they were not too severe, and we got rid of them at a fairly fast pace. Living in as close quarters as we do now, we do pass on our ailments to one another quickly, much as children do when they catch something from each other. We hope you weren't too worried, as we must make allowances for the unforeseen.

Your last letter, with the enclosed picture, was of great joy to us; to see how you have grown in both size and spirit. It reflected your ever widening scope of learning, and your growing understanding of the human problems. The fact that the school picked you to be a translator for visitors is another compliment to your sense of responsibility, and can only lead to the expansion of your bright future. As I have often said, you can never learn too much: Leave yourself open to all learning wherever it comes your way. Pursue it as you do your sports, with the same spirit of fair-mindedness.

A few days ago, we had a grand snowfall, to the delight of the sledders. Unfortunately, it has all disappeared, and there isn't enough ice to go skating. Ruth has her skates hanging outside the door in the spirit of wishful thinking; I'm sure she will get another chance to use them.

Meanwhile, we have had mail from Elsie as well as from Uncle Julius in St. Charles, and we hope they can accomplish something soon. I am a patient man, but it hurts to see Mamma and Ruth become so despondent. We lost one of our good neighbors last week, and that adds to the sadness of our present situation. As to your question about sending newspapers or magazine articles, please don't. It is not advisable, you understand. Your letters of hope are enough. We must discern for ourselves what truth is and what propaganda is. We have had slow going with our English lessons, due to the many uncertainties of our status, but I am sure, we'll catch up one day soon.

We said goodbye to the Wawern/Trier relatives. Although they are ready to go, they still have not received their final permission. The Osthofen family has arrived in Rio de Janeiro and is overjoyed at the difference in their lives. They have an opportunity to go into the fine jewelry business, thanks to a distant cousin of theirs.

And so, for today, we again have been all over the world. As armchair travelers, we do very well. Please write Gerda, and call the Chicago relatives, if you can't get to see them.

Receive our love and kisses, Your Affectionate Dad

That time in my memory ...

Everything seemed to be contingent on Uncle Julius's emerging business in St. Charles, Illinois. Although it was too early to tell, Pappa, as usual, is still optimistic about the success of getting the necessary papers to emigrate.

South America, at this moment, seemed to offer greater business opportunities in certain fields than the United States, as we still suffered from the effects of the Great Depression. The relatives going to Brazil and Argentina all made marvelous business connection. My sister, Gerda, was still torn between the offer ready for her in Brazil, and her desire to find something suitable in the United States. The opportunities to study in Brazil seemed to be much greater than those in the United States, with the people willing to sponsor her more readily. Here, she would have to study her medical sciences all over again, whereas in Brazil, they would accept what she already knew.

Here, we were all excited about Uncle Harry being asked to the inauguration, since President Roosevelt was reelected. I wished we could all go, but Uncle Harry promised us all souvenirs of the event. Although President Roosevelt was very popular with the US Jewish population, his State Department representatives in Germany were not at all. I think they played God with the unfortunate refugees, casually choosing as to who was to live and who was to die. It reminded me of the Yom Kippur Prayers we say every year, where God records the future for everyone. It seemed to me that few of them remembered the Emma Lazarus poem inscribed at the base of our Statue of Liberty: "Give me your tired, your poor, your huddled masses yearning to breathe free, the wretched refuse of your teeming shores, send these, the homeless tempest tossed to me—I lift my lamp beside the Golden Door ..."

29

March 1937

HEADLINES OF THE DAY:

SPAIN—Hemingway Reports on Decisive Battle in Brihuega, Spain

WASHINGTON—Secretary of State Hull Apologizes to German Reich for Insults by NY Mayor LaGuardia

NEW YORK—Remington Rand Company Defies National Labor Relations Board, Refuses to Re-hire 4,000 Strikers

UNITED STATES—Swastikas painted on New York Synagogues

UNITED STATES—Texas School Fire Kills 500 Children

March 9, 1937

Dearest Daughter,

We were truly pleased to receive your letter from the 22nd of February, since we hadn't heard in two weeks. No doubt, the circumstances brought other priorities in your busy life. Meanwhile, Elsie wrote that you had visited her, and the two of you caught up on all the family events. It was so nice you celebrated Purim together.

The copy of your grades pleased us very much. That you have become so knowledgeable in your second language has amazed us as well as your former teachers, and spurred us on to continue our own learning of English through the language cards you send us. They are a big help, even though they are meant for teaching youngsters.

What will you be doing over Easter? I forgot; it is not the end of the school year as it is here, but rather a break in the semester only. We shall be visiting the Erlenbacher family again, and are looking forward to it. A vacation in the country with spring coming really lifts our spirit.

The weather has been abominable, unable to decide between the last snows of winter and the chilly rain gusts of spring.

Mamma wants to write you, no doubt to ask about the family who had in mind sending for Ruth about a year ago. Could you find out more about it? She is really depressed since we were turned down by the consulate and wants Ruth out of here as soon as possible. Hearing of cousin Gretel's brilliant marriage to a United States official, much older than she, made her aware of her own inability to provide for all her children. Please try to write a cheery letter, just for her. Tell her more about your participation in the arts and music, she will really like that.

As always, Your Devoted Father

That time in my memory ...

The postponement at the consulate was again shattering. I sometimes wondered if they shouldn't have applied for Brazil, but it was out of the question: They were determined to be with me.

I hated to tell them that, although it had been fashionable to adopt a refugee child when I arrived, many people had since turned to other interests to fulfill their charitable obligations.

Mamma's migraines seemed to be getting worse. We cannot attribute them to anything other than the extreme tension of the family's situation. As it had happened before, I developed all sorts of unexplainable aches and pains, which the family called "growing pains." I really think that they were generated in sympathy with Mamma's afflictions.

School, of course was as always the relief from the family tensions with all its experimental innovations. The arts programs through the WPA were the best.

I was also becoming somewhat interested in politics, as so many of Uncle Harry's friends were in that field, and he had been invited to the inauguration. Some of the names meant very little to me, but in retrospect, they loom large on the political horizon along with President Roosevelt. Our civics class offered excellent opportunities for debate, and although the Democrats had a good voice, we were outnumbered by the Conservatives who make up most of the families along the North Shore. Just being able to express one's thoughts and beliefs was an unbelievable and exhilarating experience for someone coming from the fear-ridden restrictions of Europe.

March 31, 1937

Dear Thea,

We received your letter in Erlenbach, not realizing, although you had their [the relatives'] address, you would not send it here directly. Hope you are over your illness and that we are in touch again. Elsie said you looked like a proper invalid, with the tea cookies and nose drops when she visited you, and that your foster family was so welcoming and considerate.

Our holidays were both happy and sad. G-d only knows how many more we can celebrate with the relatives, and when we can finally celebrate them with you.

In your last letter you still gave us your old Highland Park address. We assumed that you had already moved to the new house. How different our moves are—you, to a lovely new future while we are retrenching to a questionable one. I am still hopeful as to our ability to be together by the next Seder. The relatives will combine their efforts for another affidavit. Gerda is also still waiting, and her chances for Brazil are much better than the U.S.A., as she has been requested by several doctors. Please answer Mamma's questions as to the possibility of Ruth now coming over on her own. We are very anxious as you can imagine. She is not enjoying school anymore, even though your old teachers treat her fairly and do not ignore her as some of the newly indoctrinated ones do. We feel it's only a matter of time before she is expelled.

Please let us hear about your latest move and send us your new address. Glencoe seems much closer to your school, but not very much so. You say for Easter you are visiting a campmate in Omaha, Nebraska. From what I can see on the map, it is quite far from Chicago, so will you have enough time to visit? Is your Easter holiday that long?

The relatives are all sending their love. They too are overwhelmed at all that is constantly happening in your young life. Please don't make us wait too long for another letter. Every sign of life from you is so important.

Your Loving Dad and Family

That time in my memory ...

The fact that once more I was moving to a lovely home while my parents were retrenching in theirs, left me aching and depressed. For the first time my grades slipped, but I didn't tell Pappa. I looked forward to visiting my camp-mate in Omaha, although that turned out to be a snow-bound disaster when we couldn't get out of the paralyzed city at the scheduled time.

As for moving into our new home … As much as I was excited about it, I could not get into the full spirit of anticipation, since I knew my parents were retrenching into a home scarcely bigger than my new private quarters. Mamma had to sell much of her beloved furniture that she had hoped to bring with her. I particularly remember a mahogany breakfront with beveled glass doors. It held all the lovely "forget-me-not" china that she inherited from her mother. There were Meissen dolls, Rosenthal plates, and Repoussee silver—all treasures of a well-to-do German home.

Years later, I saw some of these items in a German antique shop. I became physically ill at the thought of what Jewish home they may have come from. At least the Nazis didn't take them from her, as it was the case in so many cities. Imagine: Items that had been in families for generations were labeled "illegally obtained", and confiscated by the state.

I think it was the reluctance to part with family treasures that sealed the fate of so many people who waited far too long before trying to get out. In the end they lost everything including their lives.

30

April 1937

HEADLINES OF THE DAY:

SPAIN—German Bombers Devastate Guernica as Hundreds Die

UNITED STATES—Thomas Mann, Exiled German Writer, Pleads for Preservation of German Culture

DETROIT—Tear Gas Routs 150 Sit-Down Strikers

UNITED STATES—New U.S. Warplane "The Flying Fortress" Seen for the First Time

UNITED STATES—Pam Am Clipper Arrives in Hong Kong Marking First Commercial Flight across Pacific

April 13, 1937

Dear Thea,

Although we have just received your letter, I want to answer it immediately for many reasons. In all the time we have been writing back and forth, I have never had to reproach you for neglect or careless behavior. I must do so now.

We visited Aunt Adele last Saturday. She complained bitterly about your negligent behavior on the occasion of their visit to Chicago. Although you promised to visit them at the relatives, you failed to do so, and you failed to contact them at this very opportune time. I am sure your foster parents did not condone this; however, you alone can know the reasons, and we cannot sit in judgment about it.

As for the second request: In the past I had asked you not to approach the Perlsteins about furnishing us with affidavits, but I must ask you to do so now, as their help is urgent. I have explored every other avenue open to me, to no avail.

Equally frustrating is the inability to find an adoptive family for Ruth. Her anguish of having no one to play with, no outside amusement, and the threat of school expulsion bring her anxieties as bad as the thought of concentration camp itself. Please, dear child, direct your attention to these urgent matters immediately. I hope I have impressed upon you the need of these conditions without alarming you to the outcome. We are still all right, but how much longer we cannot say.

With Hitler's birthday next week, the propaganda machine is in full gear again, and the laws are ever tightening. Even the patience of Job has its limits, and I can no longer postpone the thoughts of disaster. It is uppermost in my mind, at the moment, and should be in yours, also.

Better news comes from Gerda. She will be leaving for Florianopolis, Brazil in July or August, and will have the chance to assist a doctor as well as continue her medical studies. Perhaps it will be easier for her to join us from there.

Mamma says do not send headache medicine or money, as that may be confiscated. Whatever you can send in the way of a wardrobe for Ruth will be most welcome, as are all your letters and pictures.

This letter has not been easy to write, but you are grown up enough to understand our anxieties, they have been a long time in coming. At least I hope you do.

Your Adoring Father

That time in my memory ...

In retrospect, this was the most devastating letter I received from Pappa. After so many distinct reminders time and time again not to involve the Perlsteins in the affidavit situation, he chastises me for ignoring the urgency. This really preyed on my conscience, since there were so many anxieties on my mind too. I showed this letter tearfully to Uncle Harry and Aunt Anne, who assured me that they certainly would have helped all along, had I not believed that my uncles had the affair well in hand. The upset caused me not to write for several weeks and to fear that somehow I had failed them.

I now realize the terrible pressure that caused Father to write what, for him, was a scathing letter, a fact that he acknowledged later.

Uncle Harry immediately set a plan in motion, the first step being a meeting with my sister Elsie.

As for finding a foster home for Ruth, that was a dead issue: With an affidavit provided for all of them, there would be no further need to bring Ruth over as a foster-child.

This was the time I really had to collect myself and pull myself together. Whenever I found myself in a crisis, I blot out the terror of it with beautiful images of peace and serenity like Duerer's "Violets in Moss", roses on a sun kissed wall; a pastoral scene by Watteau. I was soothed by the music of Mendelssohn or Haydn, my favorite being Gluck's opera, "Orpheus et Eurydice." My grades slipped again, this time under 3.0, and again I did not tell Pappa.

For the first time, I had nightmares about the entire family's being sent to a concentration camp—never to return.

31

May 1937

HEADLINES OF THE DAY:

UNITED STATES—Hindenburg Blows up—Pride of German Dirigible Fleet Burns at New Jersey Anchorage

ATLANTA—Margaret Mitchell Wins Pulitzer Prize for "Gone with the Wind"

ROME—Mussolini Tells Italian Jews "Back Fascism or Leave"

GREAT BRITAIN—Neville Chamberlain Becomes Prime Minister, Promises Peace in Europe

SAN FRANCISCO—200,000 Pedestrians Cross Golden Gate Bridge on its Opening Day

GREAT BRITAIN—George VI Crowned King

GERMANY—Hitler Asks Vatican to Rebuke American Cardinal for Criticism of Nazis

May 4, 1937

Dearest Thea,

We are puzzled by your long silence and hope it is only a temporary lapse. If I seemed unseemly harsh in my last letter to you, it is only because the urgency made me less than my usual hopeful self.

As for your hesitancy to write with all your continued optimism, do not stop that. I hate to think that I was the cause of it. Our relationship has always been so open and joyful, that I can't imagine it being otherwise. You are fully aware of the real situation now, and that is really all that matters.

I am indeed grateful that you brought Uncle Harry Perlstein together with Elsie, and that he will provide the necessary affidavits for us. Please point out to him, however, besides our deepest thanks for his generosity, he will not be held responsible for any future contribution to our livelihood. Once we are there, Mamma and I will both have waiting jobs through Uncle Ernest, so the Perlsteins will have no further financial obligation. The fact that they want to keep you with them is making us, more than ever, grateful to them.

Ruth has also some good news in her future. She is being sent to Switzerland for a month's vacation, rest, and recuperation through a Jewish relief agency. We are all looking forward to it, as it will be easier to relocate into the new apartment that is being readied for us. We should be as comfortable as possible in the four rooms allotted to the family. It will seem strange to pay rent on my own house.

By then, you too, will have moved on a somewhat grander scale, but with a real look to the future. We can't wait for further pictures of the new surroundings with all their luxurious beauty.

Gerda is moving to Hamburg, where she is engaged as an X-ray technician in the Jewish hospital which is still flourishing. She feels very fortunate that whatever agreement Wolfgang made with the regime, it guaranteed her safety and ability to continue her medical studies.

The last of the Jewish children have moved from Eisenberg, so in order to play with anyone we must take Ruth to Grünstadt, but there, too, the children are leaving.

I'm sorry the family that wanted her at one time is no longer interested, but as you said there is no longer that first enthusiasm that came with your emigration.

G-d bless you and all those who are trying to help. It is of great comfort to us, and we shall try to be patient a little longer.

Your Loving Dad

That time in my memory ...

Naturally my silence had been due to the shock of Pappa's letter of April 13th. I could not respond to this scolding. My letters following his admonition were more cautious and sober, and not as full of enthusiasm as before. There are times when your instincts tell you it is better to be a less heedful child than is demanded of you, and this was definitely one of those times. I regret to this day not having followed my instincts. Such a waste of precious time, such a useless time spent on anxieties

Nevertheless, I was very happy to hear of Ruth's good luck getting a vacation in Switzerland. That and the cooperation of Uncle Harry on the affidavit situation opened communications with Pappa again.

My relief was indescribable. It was awesome to behold Uncle Harry going into action, and taking over the situation. With his positive assurances and indomitable energy, I felt sure that this time we would succeed.

32

June 1937

HEADLINES OF THE DAY:

FRANCE—Former British King, Now Duke of Windsor, Marries American Divorcee

UNITED STATES—CIO Seizes Lansing, Michigan, Plant to Protest Arrest of Pickets

JERUSALEM—Royal Commission Considers Partition of Palestine between Jews and Arabs

HOLLYWOOD—Platinum Blonde Jean Harlow, Movie Idol, Dies

MOSCOW—Eight Soviet Generals Shot

UNITED STATES—Joe Louis Beats Braddock in 7 Rounds to Become World Heavyweight Champion

BERLIN—150,000 German War Veterans Cheer King George VI during State Visit

June 8, 1937

Dear Thea,

We received your letters on our return from Monzernheim and were greatly relieved since we heard nothing for almost three weeks.

Although you wrote very little about your post-confirmation celebration, we are sure it was a lovely event. We were delighted to hear that the entire family was on hand to celebrate it with you. We enjoyed the special poem Aunt Frances Perlstein wrote for the occasion. Elsie and Grandmother wrote they were able to be there, and that Elsie is now companion and caretaker for Grandfather Agazim. In her last letter she mentioned nothing more about her meeting with Uncle Harry Perlstein and the state of our papers, but we're assuming by all calculations that we are right on track again, and should be asked to the consulate by July, August the latest.

Dear Ruth is already in Switzerland for three weeks and enjoying it very much. At least, on her return, she can correspond with the children she met there and won't be so lonely anymore. We are keeping the letter you wrote her until she returns, as she will be back next week. Then our little apartment will be lively again.

Dear Gerda is in Hamburg, where she is working in the X-ray department of the hospital. She will be coming home for a farewell visit, as she will embark for South America by mid-July. The voyage will take the small steamer 18 to 20 days and should be relaxing for her after all she has been through.

We presume your long vacation has started and that you will have a most enjoyable one. You are not as enthusiastic as you have been in the past; why is that? It sounds exciting that you are going on a countrywide trip with Aunt Frances. You will see so much more of the U.S., have new experiences, and make many more friends.

In all the excitement, I've forgotten to ask about your foot injury. I'm sure you'll be back on your horse, and all the other activities you're involved in before you know it.

There is still a note of sadness in your letter, and I hope it soon will disappear. You will miss your camp-mates this summer, but growing up means the faces around us change from time to time, but that doesn't mean that feelings will.

You didn't mention what sort of report card you received, I'm sure it was excellent.

We are having a terrible hailstorm at the moment. I hate to think what it will do to the beautiful summer harvest. We are due to pick cherries and early peas next week. As you can see, I have become quite a farmer.

The relatives in Monzernheim sent their warmest greetings. It is good we have such an extended family where we can visit as in the days past, and forget the ever-threatening future for a little while.

With deep affection—Your Loving Family, Your Daddy

That time in my memory ...

After my confirmation, the Perlstein family had another celebration to commemorate the day. I was still suffering from depression after Daddy's scolding, so this event was a happy change for me. I still did not write him about my grades slipping, and I begged Aunt Anne not to either.

Aunt Frances, who was Uncle Harry's sister, had offered to take me on an extended trip throughout northern Michigan as my confirmation present from him. This was to be my summer vacation instead of camp. She was a lovely lady, and a poetess of some note. Having lived all over the world, she still made Chicago her home when she returned from her travels. Slight of stature, she was nevertheless, a bundle of energy, ever exploring the new and the untried. She wrote ferociously, and I have at least five of her published books of poetry. I was really flattered and delighted by her offer. We were to go to Mackinac Island in Michigan, where I could ride my bike everywhere, as no cars were permitted on the island. Aunt Frances also taught me something I've never forgotten. She said: "Wherever you go in the world, take something near and dear to you along: a picture, a lamp, a vase. That way you will never feel alone and strange." As a world traveler she would certainly advise me well. It has certainly worked for me in my global wanderings over the years from Japan to Germany.

33

July 1937

HEADLINES OF THE DAY:

UNITED STATES—Amelia Earhart Disappears in Flight over Pacific Ocean

GERMANY—Pastor Niemöller, Leading German Lutheran Churchman, Jailed for Resisting Nazis

LONDON—American Don Budge Becomes First Player to Win Singles, Doubles, and Mixed at Wimbledon

CHINA—Japanese Rout Chinese Troops with Tanks and Bombers from Peking and Tientsin

BELFAST—King George VI Escapes I.R.A. Bombs

LONDON—Prime Minister Chamberlain Sends Note to Mussolini as "Peace Gesture"

July 4, 1937

Dearest Thea,

Today is the 4th of July, an important holiday for everyone in the United States of America. I wish we could enjoy it with you; but definitely next year. Where the final prayer at the Seder is "Next year in Jerusalem!" ours is a fervent "Next year in the United States!"

I am sure you are enjoying your trip with Aunt Frances, who sounds like a delightful lady. Her travels around the world and her poetry make her sound like someone who enjoys life to the fullest. It is interesting that you showed her some of Ruth's little poems and she liked them, but our little poet has a long way to go.

You have probably received your grades, and I assume you've reached the desired "4.0" again, since you mentioned a junior scholarship at the Art Institute. That is a wonderful accomplishment.

Dear Ruth returned from Switzerland last Thursday, and we hardly knew her. She had gained five pounds, was as brown as a berry, and cheerful as a squirrel. Your old camp uniforms were a wonderful addition to her wardrobe, since it gave her a real feeling of being in a summer camp as you were. As you know, here we have other camps, and they are not very pleasant for those who are in them. The latest to join them is Pastor Niemöller who has resisted the Nazis for so long. May G-d bless him and keep him safe.

Gerda has been here since Sunday, and though we are overjoyed at her good luck, we are sad at the thought of her leaving again. She and Mamma are in Monzernheim, but will be back in time to add to this letter. I am alone as Ruth went to Grünstadt, where she now must go for her religious lessons. With the limited space we have, I will not have her taught the Good Book in the kitchen. Besides, the Cantor is afraid to travel away from home, so this is a better arrangement. So alone, I have time to think and hopefully plan ahead.

I fear I have somehow built a wall between us. Was it that in my anxiety that I berated you? Please be open with me, as you would with Gerda, who also senses a reticence in your last letters.

Here it has been very hot. For us that means plenty of walks in the cool green woods close by and the gathering of blueberries and pinecones. Mamma would like to make some wreaths for goodbyes to our loyal neighbors.

I am still busy writing travel tickets and insurance for people. I wish it were my own.—

Your Ever Devoted Dad

That time in my memory ...

As I mentioned before, my grades had slipped, though I did not reveal this to my Dad. Since I had received the Junior Scholarship at the Art Institute, I was able to overcome that disappointment. I was delighted that Ruth had such a wonderful time in Switzerland, and, again, it relieved me of my enduring feelings of guilt on her account.

I could not comment on Dad's observation as to the wall between us, and that Gerda too was conscious of it. I knew that it would take time to get over it.

His news about Pastor Niemöller saddened me. The Pastor had always stood for righteousness, and his courage was an inspiration to all. What was happening to all the righteous people of Germany? Were they all destined to perish for their beliefs?

The 4th of July is always a day of joy and celebration—this was no exception. The house was filled with guests who enjoyed the yearly hospitality ending up with the fireworks at the club.

Our spirits were somewhat dampened by the news that my idolized Amelia Earhart was lost at sea on her round the world trip. I could not imagine someone of her experience and expertise could have mysteriously disappeared at sea. There were all kinds of speculative rumors. What devastated me was the fact that she was the first of many women that opened my eyes to their place in U.S. history, and now she was lost. Flying was something new and exhilarating for me, and I had several rides at Glenview airport with a friend of Uncle Harry. Here again my youthful enthusiasm placed it on my list as a goal of future accomplishment.

Letter from Gerda:

July 4, 1937

Dearest Sister Thea,

We've just returned from our farewell to the Monzernheimer relatives, but it was in great spirits as we will be united again in Brazil. The boys will be in the jewelry trade there, and I will have the continuation of my studies.

I should be angry with you, for being such a lazy writer with all that is happening to you, but I'm not ... I'm too happy about the future.

I will be leaving here Monday and will embark on the 16th of July, the day before your 15th birthday. I know it will be a special day for you, full of gifts and celebrations. Please write me about it.

Pappa says you have been reluctant to write with your former enthusiasm. He fears he was too harsh on you. Please don't let it destroy your feelings of joy in everything you do. You are a good and thoughtful girl, aware of your responsibility more than most. I know things are underway for their exit visas, but continue to encourage them with all the good that lies in wait for them over there.

You still don't know what you want to study toward a career. There is still time, but if you want medicine you must go heavy into sciences quite soon. Let me know what your feelings are toward the field I have chosen.

Eisenberg is not the same anymore. Most of the young men are gone and, except for a few, most of the young women show little interest in study. Their work is keeping a home and raising children for the Führer. I am glad I left it behind and wish with all my heart that the parents can do so, very soon.

I must go to Ludwigshafen to pick up some equipment for the hospital, so until you write me in Brazil, I send you love with all my heart. Keep me in yours, until we meet again. Grow as you have been doing in mind, in spirit, and in body.

As always, Your Loving Gerda

That time in my memory ...

Gerda's optimistic letter helped much in my healing process. I hoped with all my summer activities, I could get back to the former relationship that I had enjoyed with my father. I was happy that Brazil seemed to point the way to Gerda's future medical career, and that so many people there were interested in her future.

As for me, I knew that I was not cut out for the same career, but determined to pursue the Arts. My Saturday scholarship at the Art Institute was a great encouragement and so were my other artistic interests. Though, I was not planning to go to camp that summer, there were a whole slew of out door activities. The crowning glory of them was the season ticket to Ravinia—the beautiful summer residence of the Chicago Symphony Orchestra. Ravinia was just to the north of us and close enough that you could hear some of the magnificent music.

July 18, 1937

Dear Thea,

We received your letter from the 8th of July, noting that you had to postpone your trip with Aunt Frances because you were ill. Hopefully it is nothing serious. I am sure Mrs. Perlstein would have informed us if it were. It was somewhat alarming that it involved an overnight stay at a hospital. If we had telephone privileges, we would call immediately. Perhaps you can call Mr. Heilmann, and he can relay the message to us. We are anxious to hear what happened.

Gerda has left and will have quite an adventure in traveling, first by ship to Rio, then a day's trip by train to San Francisco du Sol, followed by a day's trip by car to Florianopolis. We hope to hear only good news from her from here on in. I accompanied her to Frankfurt where I had some business and had a wonderful visit with the Herz family. It is wonderful to have friends in places where we spent such happy times.

The house is totally altered, and now holds seven families. We are still lucky to have the bathroom, now remodeled into a kitchen and bath, and what was Grandfather's study and bedroom. So we still have a place to keep our books and family memorabilia. The synagogue is also an apartment, and I'm sure the Nazi family that moved into it does not appreciate that.

At the moment we are all terribly sad. We just brought Anna Pahler to her final rest. It is a blessing that she is released from her long suffering and is no longer a burden to her family. Lenchen wants to come with us to the U.S. and work as Mamma's maid, but that is impossible. We could not afford to pay her U.S. wages. There is so much sadness here, but like Job we shoulder it for G-d's sake, as well as our own.

Although you forgot Mamma's birthday, we sent you our belated greetings to yours. We will celebrate all of them when we get together.

Your Ever Devoted Dad.

That time in my memory …

A thyroid problem sent me to the hospital for an overnight stay, and a postponement of my vacation trip with Aunt Frances. The telephone was a last resort measure, but we were reluctant to use it. With the government monitoring all overseas calls, we did not want to get Mr. Heilmann into trouble with the authorities.

Gerda really embarked on quite an adventure. Imagine that in this day and age, such a long trek from one civilized country to another halfway around the world took 20 days.

Pappa mentioned that they did not get the former synagogue as part of their apartment. I knew that this was a great disappointment to all of them. I know it was to me. Still, they were comfortable in Grandfather's old suite.

In reference to Anna Pahler, she was Lenchen's sister, and as a tuberculosis patient, suffered many years as a bed-ridden invalid. She was a lovely, patient girl who spent those years doing exquisite embroidery. I always think of her when I see and hear "La Bohème." The compulsion to identify her with the tragic Mimi is irresistible.

Sadly, she never had the tragic romance in her life as Mimi did. I wish Mamma could have brought Lenchen with her. She would have been such a staunch, wonderful support for her, but the wage problems in the United States would be insurmountable.

I was still planning my trip with Aunt Frances. In addition to Mackinac Island, we planned to visit an artist friend of hers in Saginaw, Michigan. Aunt Frances was, of course, delighted that I had chosen art as my major interest and knew the works of many artists, both here and abroad. My studies at Chicago Art Institute would certainly broaden my horizon as well as familiarize me with leading American Artists about whom, at that time, I knew very little. Going to Northwestern would really broaden my career aspect in that field.

34

August 1937

HEADLINES OF THE DAY:

MOSCOW—Thirty Churchmen Put on trial, Accused of "Plotting with Fascist Governments"

BERLIN—Official Teaching Manual Issued, Stresses Need for Preaching Anti-Semitism

CHINA—Japan Occupies Capital at Peking, Sets up Army Rule

CHINA—U.S. Cruiser "Augusta" Hit by Japanese Shell at Shanghai: One Dead, 19 Hurt

PALESTINE—Jews Ask for Direct Negotiations with Arabs before Partition of Palestine

Erlenbach, August 1, 1937

Dearest Thea,

We received your letter, forwarded to Erlenbach, and are relieved to learn that you are up and about again. Mamma and I are here, and Ruth went to visit in Schwegenheim, where there are more children to play with and more activities for her to pursue.

It sounds like great excitement with an attempted break-in at the new house, but the good Arnold had it all under control, as you wrote us. You never mentioned before that he was a Chicago policeman assigned to the family, but it is very comforting to know. No wonder he always wants to know where you are going and what you are doing. That is part of his job. It sounds as though you are well protected.

Finally, we received the wonderful news that the Consulate has received our papers and, except for a few minor technicalities, we should be there by the end of the month. It cannot happen fast enough, as living here with six other families is most strained and uncomfortable. At least they are polite, and not antagonistic.

We had visitors from Landstuhl. Since Gretel's new husband is in politics in the U.S., he is moving heaven and earth to get them their papers for emigration. They may have their exit visas before we do. That would be quite ironic, but we must accept the reality of it.

I apologize that I assumed you forgot Mamma's birthday, and we thank you in advance for all that is waiting for us at home.

The weather for the harvest was beautiful; the healthy hard work made us forget our troubles and made the reward of a good meal all the more enjoyable. With the news from the Consulate, Mamma is much happier and no longer complains of her devastating migraines as before.

We had a visit from a young man who told us that he used to write to you, but you never answered back. He was interested in what had become of you in the United States and that you were doing well. He sends greetings, and was very sorry he could not continue to write. After his Grandfather died, he had joined the "Jugenddienst" (the young people's labor group).

We hope you can resume your vacation plans with Aunt Frances. The island where you are going sounds beautiful. Imagine … no car traffic, only bicycles, just like in Holland. We know you will enjoy it. Write us a postcard from there and wherever else you are going. Ruth loves to collect them.

Meanwhile, our love to you. It won't be much longer now. We're having a thorough physical examination when we get home and my eye operation should present no problems. With love from all the relatives—

Your Devoted Father

That time in my memory ...

The attempted "break-in" at the new house was just a malfunctioning of the security system, some leaves drifting across the sensitive window detectors. Since the Lindbergh kidnapping, however, many well-to-do families received police protection, and Arnold Lieberman provided that for us loyally over many years.

The crisis over the exit visas seemed to be over, and all was back on track for my family's speedy exit from Nazi Germany. I can see where living with six other families in a government-enforced relationship was not easy, particularly in the small space allotted them.

The young man who called on them in Erlenbach was the boy who had sent me the letters and poetry after my last summer there. I felt very badly that now he could no longer explore the poetry of Heinrich Heine, certainly not in the Jugenddienst.

The island that Dad spoke of was Mackinac Island where I had hoped to forget the recent upsets in the company of Aunt Frances. As I mentioned before, we were to stay with an artist friend of hers in Saginaw which is quite an art community in Michigan. I looked forward to learning more about current American Artists as those I was familiar with amounted to very few: Hopper, Bellows, Sargent, Cassatt, Grant Woods, and Thomas Hart Benton. Americans as a whole still didn't appreciate the wonderful artists who produced work of importance at that time and still collected major works from Europe. With the expansion of the WPA, there was an ever widening exposure to American Art which was badly needed. Now there was greater concentration on American Artists and what they were painting—Life in America.

August 24, 1937

Dear Daughter Thea,

I am really concerned about your lack of communication with us over the past five weeks. Since your July letters, there have been no others from you. We are leaving for Schwegenheim on Monday and shall be there over the Holidays, which means another wait for your letters. I had left instructions to forward all mail, but obviously this is not being done. I know you may be on vacation, but there should be no lack of communication at this crucial time in our lives. Our official papers have caught up with us: why not your letters? You had promised to write every week or two, which seems like a reasonable request. My dear child, I don't think we asked too much of you, you have never failed us in our request.

But, enough of my complaints about the situation.

The wonderful news is that we have been requested to be at the Consulate on the 13th of September. At long last! We hope that all goes well, and by my reckoning we should be in the United States by the end of November/beginning of December. I dare not think of how much worse it will become for the Jews in Germany this coming year. There is a rumor that they will be relocated in new concentration camps for their own "protection and welfare."

Gerda arrived in Florianopolis, Brazil after a 20 day voyage, but her first letter via the newly established air route between Germany and Brazil took only four days. That is progress in our modern world as we know it.

We will celebrate Rosh Hashanah, the New Year, with the relatives, perhaps for the last time. May you celebrate them with a wish for all our well-being. It has been a long three years for us, years of heartaches and pain. For you it has passed, I am sure, in the blinking of an eye.

Once more we shall take up our English lessons with new enthusiasm and hope. We send our thanks, blessings, and good wishes to your foster parents and all they are doing for of us.

Please write soon and remember us in your Rosh Hashanah prayers.

Your Devoted Daddy

That time in my memory ...

At last! The visit to the Consulate had become a reality, and this time, I was sure the results would be positive. Somehow, having Uncle Harry in the picture made it a most reassuring sign that all would go well. I was particularly anxious since I had heard that the Nazis had opened another concentration camp at Buchenwald. This one was for political prisoners and homosexuals, as well as the now "stateless" Germans, meaning, of course, the Jews. So it was a relief to hear that the family actually had a date for a consulate interview. I cannot thank Uncle Harry and Governor Horner enough for coming to their rescue. I don't know who of Uncle Harry's political friends were involved, but I'm eternally grateful to all of them. Politics here leaves me in awe, but not with the crippling fear as in Germany.

I was looking forward to a whole new school curriculum as a sophomore, with many more experimental opportunities for learning. My assigned pen pals in French class lived in Carcassonne, in the south of France. They were just as eager to learn English as I was to learn French. Having been French or Alsatian on Mother's side made the connection so much more familiar and offered a ready-made opportunity for an easy exchange of experiences. Sad to say, nobody had any German pen pals. German was not being offered as a language option. With the present ideology and the indoctrination of students there, it would be impossible to establish a rapport. That was a pity.

35

September 1937

HEADLINES OF THE DAY:

GERMANY—Nazis Open Fourth Concentration Camp at Buchenwald

NUREMBERG—Nazis Hold Biggest Party Rally in Nuremberg

WASHINGTON—Labor Leader John L. Lewis warns FDR to Back C.I.O. or Lose Labor Support

WASHINGTON—U. S. Ships Forbidden to Transport Arms to Far East

PALESTINE—Andrew Lewis, Chief of British Peace Legation, Killed by Arabs

GERMANY—Hitler and Mussolini Sign Munich Pact of Non-Aggression

September 8, 1937

Dearest Daughter,

Mail is finally catching up with us, including the postcards from your vacation. You are learning a lot about U.S. geography, traveling from one end of the country to another. Mackinac Island, in upper Michigan, sounds very much like Northern Europe, Denmark, Norway, Sweden, or Finland. The fact that you visited a Finnish family bears that out. What is interesting is that there are no automobiles on the island; that's unusual for America with all its automobiles.

Now, you will be starting your second year of High School with many new subjects, including much more French as your language. I am sure, you will speak three languages well by the time you are finished. Many of the words will be familiar to you, as Grandfather spoke a *patois*, a mixture of German and French words—the language of Strassburg in Alsace-Lorraine.

We will be going home after the holidays. Ruth's vacation will also be over, and she will meet us there.

We were lucky to get all the harvest in, as it suddenly turned quite cold. The winter clothes you are sending for Ruth should fit her very well, since she grew so much on her vacation in Switzerland.

I have written my first long English letter to Mr. Perlstein, thanking him for providing the necessary papers. I also assured him that he would be in no way responsible for our maintenance and well-being once we are over there. That will be a matter to work out between the uncles.

I am only sorry that the family who was so eager for Ruth last year is no longer interested. Under the new development, we'll manage very well all the same.

In anticipation of seeing you again, the family is full of plans. We hope you are too. Write soon.

Sending you our love,

Your Dad, Mamma, and Little Sister

That time in my memory ...

Mackinac was a delight and truly revived my spirits. The people were so hospitable. We stayed at a lovely hotel with wide, white-stained, clapboard verandas by every room. Aunt Frances knew so may people. Some were there for only the summer, but many remained in year-long residence. Quite an undertaking when you think of the harsh, blustering winters on the lakes. But we were far from that—there were picnics, poetry readings in the evening and "homemade" musicals. The latter, though not particularly professional, were nevertheless emotionally stirring and endearing. I didn't read a newspaper in all the time we visited there, and thus kept all my anxieties at bay.

I couldn't bear to hear the word "Germany" or see the swastika without my heart beating rapidly with fear, particularly since these signs had now also appeared in our own Madison Square Garden and New York synagogues. Father Coughlin, a Catholic priest, shouted his anti-Semitic tirades over the airwaves, and the Ku Klux Klan preached its version of racial purity, all under the banner of America, the land of free speech.

Some how I felt it can't happen here, that I was safe. I had that faith in the American people that they would not be misled by the demagogues of hate. Still, there was a chilling reaction in me that is automatic. But all that seemed a lifetime away from our Middle America summer. On our way back we stopped with Tagne's (our nursemaid) family in Holland, Michigan and again with Aunt Frances's friend in Saginaw, where there was a whole new world of creative work for me to study and admire.

September 20, 1937

Dear Daughter,

It is hard to believe that last week we were at the Consulate, and how smooth everything ran. The fact that Uncle Harry and his friend, the former Governor, vouched for me made all the difference in the world. Even the question of my eye operation was never raised.

We enjoyed a wonderful visit with your sponsors in Stuttgart, and they were delighted how well you are doing. Their son has arranged for them to emigrate from Germany to South America, while he will negotiate for Jews with a committee from Sweden, and remain in Europe. He is a very brave young man. So are Mr. Heilmann's son and nephew, who both have been sent to "re-education" camps for "dissenters."

With your new school subjects, you sound as if you are at school from early morning to late in the afternoon: 9 AM to 5 PM sounds like a very long time. It is good you do not have to take the train all the time; that the dependable Arnold picks you up. I do, however, feel 16 years old is too young to learn to drive a car. Do your foster parents know he is teaching you? I suppose as a policeman he is a very responsible teacher, but please do not do anything rash.

Your Saturdays—filled with art and music—sound so satisfying. I suppose I must resign myself to the fact that you will not study medicine. There is still much time to decide, but a career in the arts is very uncertain. But I suppose the satisfaction outweighs the uncertainty.

We are already feeling signs of winter, but feel we have enough provisions to last, should we have to wait it out. I have told you that many young educated Jews are taking up farming to the point that they are establishing an agricultural school in Hamburg for preparing them to immigrate to Palestine. That is the only positive thing I have heard of lately.

We send you all our love. Although things are moving, do not stop writing your weekly letters.

Until the next letter—Your Daddy

That time in my memory ...

Things were beginning to move quite quickly, since their visit to the Consulate. Reflecting on Dad's remark about young Mr. Neuberger, the son of my sponsors in Stuttgart, I wondered if he was not on the Raoul Wallenberg committee, which helped the Jews of Europe to escape the Holocaust.

The Agricultural School in Hamburg, surprisingly enough, was endorsed by the Nazi German government, because they felt that it encouraged Jews to leave Germany and settle in another country; anything that helped to get rid of Jews was tacitly or explicitly approved by the Nazis.

Learning to drive was something I did with pride, just like riding a horse. Unfortunately, it did not continue past the first few lessons, as a dear young friend of mine was killed in a tragic accident on her 16th birthday. She was a cautious driver, and my foster parents trusted her driving; it gave us both such a sense of freedom and independence. We could now go places at night without an adult driving us.

One incident that stands out was the "independence on wheels", a night at Teatro de Lago, the movie palace in No Mans Land between Winnetka and Kenilworth. It was one of the earliest shopping centers. The development was one of pink-Floridian architecture that gave you a sense of being in Florida. It was a tropical adventure to go to a "beachcomber" restaurant, visit exotic shops and go to the movies at Teatro de Lago with its palm trees tropic decor. On our night of independence we saw a sinister Charlie Chan film through the last performance and found ourselves the only two people remaining in the audience. Too frightened to approach the night watchman, we huddled in the car—only to find in our panic that it wouldn't start! As the only car in the parking lot we did attract the night guards' attention, and they duly informed our families where we were. As always, Arnold came to the rescue and, much abashed, we promised no more nighttime excursions alone.

Driving opened up a whole new world of activities, particularly at Northwestern University, where Pearl's brother was a student, and where cultural events abounded. Though we were years younger, he generously invited us to many of the student activities and we were flattered that he recognized our maturity. The fact that I was born in Europe was a plus factor with his friends. The shock of her useless, tragic death that winter kept me from driving for many years, until I was forced to learn while my husband was overseas.

I have already mentioned social activities, like concerts (where I got to know Burl Ives), the Wa-mu-shows and football games—I was fascinated with the open seminars of Bergen Evans and his sister Cornelia. I still have a book I bought at that time and continue to use it after all these years. Many years later, when I was working as a layout artist in Chicago, the studio sent me to Northwestern for the study in creative writing to help me in writing ad copy for my own layouts. Again, it was the English dynamics of Bergen Evans that came to the forefront.

It was a time when, as so often before, I was examining my own situation. One night at dinner, one of Uncle Harry's friends, a venerable judge, was discussing a new law the Nazis issued. It encompassed removing children from their parents if they *failed to teach them Nazi doctrine, and placing the children in the care of the State. I could not help but compare it with my own life, so rich and outgoing. I never felt I was taken away from my parents for any ideological reasons, just to give me the best start in life possible. When Pappa wrote me about it, I didn't believe it. Now with Judge Julius Hoffman's stating the fact, I did.*

School was exciting but for me a very long day. To make a 9AM class, I had to catch an 8AM train. With after school activities, I didn't get home until dinnertime unless Arnold picked me up. No wonder I treasured my weekends of carefree existence: meeting my friends, going to my art classes or symphony hall—that was the very positive side of my life.

A new phase was added to my Art Institute studies: We could work with the Goodman Theater group, designing scenery and helping with production. That was right up my alley—fitting into my Saturday program of activities.

36

October 1937

HEADLINES OF THE DAY:

PALESTINE—British Deport Arab Leaders

LONDON—Crowd Breaks Up Fascist Meeting, Mosley Injured

WASHINGTON—U.S. Drops Neutral Stand on China, Condemns Japan as Invader

PALESTINE—British Restrict Jewish Immigration to Palestine

ROME—Mussolini Pledges Support for Hitler's Colonial Claims

NEW JERSEY—Princeton Professor Predicts Extermination of German Jews within Ten Years

October 1, 1937

Dearest Thea,

We are writing "October 1", and fall is really upon us. It seems so normal to sit here, to hear the clock ticking and the crackling of the pinecones in the stove with rainstorms outside. Ruth and I are practicing our English vocabulary. We are also reading the book you sent, but there are many words which neither one of us know, though it is a children's book.

We've had to send in more papers, mostly doctor's certificates, that our health is good, and that none of us has tuberculosis. That is the illness that denies so many unfortunates the opportunity to emigrate.

We shall have jobs waiting for us, though we pledged not to take jobs from able-bodied Americans; that will not be the case with us. Mine will be to keep the hotel accounts, and Mamma will help with the housekeeping. We will not receive regular salaries, but will work in exchange for housing and furnishings. We shall see what else it entails when we get there.

Please keep writing, at least until the beginning of November. I think we will surely be packing by then. I wonder if the people at the Consulate are aware of the responsibility they hold over our lives—that they make decisions that shape our future for good or bad. Observing them, they don't seem to care one way or another. They have a quota to fill, and that is all.

Mamma is knitting furiously to finish a suit appropriate for traveling and, thanks to you, Ruth has a warm winter wardrobe. It doesn't really matter what we wear—the early immigrants, in their peasant clothes, weren't any more grateful and relieved than we are to be coming to America's shores.

We had an impressive funeral in Eisenberg. One of the most trusted *Gauleiters* of the Nazi regime died, and dignitaries came from all over the country for the funeral. As a former member of the city council, I was invited to the ceremony. Can you imagine the irony of that? Providentially, even the Führer cannot stop his most loyal followers from dying. It seems there is still a Higher Authority that decides our fate, and in that I trust.

With loving blessings for the coming year—may it see us reunited with you.

Your Loving Father

That time in my memory ...

Since the recent visit to the Consulate in Stuttgart, Father's mood had become positive again, and so had mine. His assessment of the Consulate staff in those days seems to have been correct, as I have learned since those days. Many had Nazi sympathies, as had a good many other people in our State Department.

Now everything was geared toward my parent's ultimate arrival in the U.S. The most important issue was that they would not be dependent on support other than my uncles. The U.S. still had a lot of recovery to do in the aftermath of the Depression, and was careful not to swell its welfare rolls with immigrants.

School was, as always, challenging, but the big concern was what I could do for them on their arrival. I made elaborate plans about what to show them when they got here.

I was making these big plans, particularly for Ruth, who had had so little to amuse her in the last three years. The Perlstein children were disappointed that she would not be coming to live with us, but I assured them that they could see her as often as they liked. I really looked forward to a close relationship between my parents and foster parents.

Only time would tell. I realized the difference in their lives up to now, but hoped their compassion and their understanding of human nature and frailty would bridge that gap.

October 15, 1937

Dearest Daughter,

I cannot tell you how fast the time seems to be going now that we know our wait is almost over.

Mamma is in the process of giving away some of the small things she has treasured, to those who have remained so faithful to us. None of them that belonged to your Grandmother; those she will bring to you.

We are not bringing many new things, as we have heard that some never reach the boat; that they are "confiscated" by helpful inspectors; that includes mostly silverware and fine china. Since most of our possessions are not in sets, we won't have to surrender two out of twelve. From what I hear, that seems to be the ratio.

You sound so busy as you are going into fall and winter with another campmate reunion in sight. This time you say it is in Louisiana, where many of the girls live. We wish you much enjoyment. We do hope you are planning your winter vacation around our arrival in Chicago, which should be early December at the latest. Ruth is very excited about you showing her the places you've talked about in your letters. I am glad you told your former sponsors, the Sonnenscheins, about our coming. Naturally we look forward to meeting them, too. It is good that you are still in touch with them, and that they are still part of your life.

We hope that you are finally over your lingering ailment, that you can once more participate in your beloved sports. I have never heard of the Indian game called Lacrosse. From your description it sounds like a game that needs great skill to play. Your drawing of the net-pocket explained much to us, but we must see it to understand how it really works. Equally mystifying is American football. Here, too, we must see it to believe it. I can see there is much to learn in America besides the language.

Mr. Heilmann's son and nephew are still in "re-education camp." I hope and pray they can come home soon, as he cannot run the newspaper alone much longer, and the state is threatening to put a "current propagandist" over the operation of the paper. It will break his heart.

Our love to you for now. As always, we pray for our soon-to-be meeting.

Your Daddy

That time in my memory ...

From many immigrants I learned of the ratio system: If you brought anything out of Germany in sets of twelve, you were "expected" to surrender two of each. To this day, I have everything in sets of ten as my mother-in-law had to turn over two of everything when she emigrated.

Mamma was able to sell our good furniture and start out here with a clean slate. I wish she could have brought some of Grandmother's pieces but they were too massive to transport. I am trying to remember my favorite pieces of china that belonged to grandmother, and I can honestly say the memory escapes me. Perhaps when I see them again they will assume their former meaning in my life.

Uncle Ernst and Aunt Lydia had made arrangements for the family to occupy a one-bedroom apartment in the hotel where they worked. It was all ready waiting for them. Ruth would be going to school nearby, and Auntie would take her. I tried to think of what I could give them by way of furniture from my room, but Aunt Anne came to the rescue with a lovely mahogany coffee table and end table set, as well as some Chippendale bookcases. My parents' and Ruth's moving into their own apartment in a free country would be a lovely occasion after all.

A word about Mr. Heilmann's young relatives who ended up in a concentration camp: The newspaper was taken over by the Nazis. Even Father learned nothing further about their fate—whether or not they ever were released. Their example is why I could never lump all Germans as Nazis, that people are either all good or all bad—that all opinions are either all positive or all negative. There are numerous and subtle gradations between the extremes.

37

November 1937

HEADLINES OF THE DAY:

UNITED STATES—NY Mayor LaGuardia Reelected in Spite of Right Wing Opposition

ITALY—Rome Joins With Berlin & Tokyo in Anti-Soviet Pact

LONDON—Lord Halifax, British Diplomat, Visits Germany, Seeks to Appease Nazis

GERMANY—Nazis Separate Parents from Children for Teaching "Non-Conformity"

MOSCOW—Soviets Celebrate 20 Years of Russian Revolution as One Million March

UNITED STATES—Armistice Day Commemorated Across the Nation

November 1, 1937

Dearest Daughter Thea,

Today is All Hallow and All Saints Day, a day for reflection and remembrance for our Christian friends. For us it is a look into what will be a better future. It is a day of a somber mood, with the weather equally sad and dreary, typical November. As for us, the sun is shining brightly, and our mood is one of hope. Even little Ruth has stopped complaining and starts each day with the chatter of things that need to be done.

Mamma is overjoyed, to be in Chicago where she can hear all the music she likes, and eat in a fine restaurant again. As for me, I close the book on what we had, what we have, and what will have. I want no hate in my heart: I'm sad only because I must leave some lasting friendships behind. G-d only knows what their lot will be in the future.

Gerda is very happy in Brazil at her new job and continuing studies. She is, however, aware of how many Nazi sympathizers there are among the German population there; but it is kept very much under wraps. In spite of it, there is not the flagrant anti-Semitism as there is here, and the new immigrants are welcome.

We had a surprise letter from a brother of Mamma's whom she had not heard from in years. I am sure you didn't even know of his family's existence. His name is Joseph, and he owns a bakery (just as Grandfather did), in upper New York. He and his family would like to welcome us when the boat arrives. That means we will not have to go through the immigration shelter.

Aunt Lydia writes that you want to be with them when they pick us up at the train station. That will be wonderful. We also thank the Perlsteins for offering us their hospitable home. We can make all these plans when we get there.

Dear child, I cannot call you that much longer, you are spreading your wings in all directions. Do not take on too many things, rather become adept in those that are comfortable and familiar to you. I know the young want to experiment and experience everything, but too many of those also have their pitfalls, and you'll find yourself drifting in too many directions. What you have is good, hold onto that.

Until the next letter—

Your Devoted Father

That time in my memory ...

As the time came closer for their arrival, I became more uneasy as more violent out-breaks against Jews took place in Germany. Even here the Nazis became bolder with meetings in Madison Square Garden, the desecration of synagogues with swastikas, and Father Coughlin's diatribes.

Then, too, I worried as to their settling in Chicago: Would our preparations really be enough? Aunt Anne sensed my uneasiness about my split future and threw a sur-prise Halloween party for me with all of my friends in attendance. It was a scavenger hunt, with clues planted all along the North Shore from the Bai Hai Temple in Wil-mette, the Teatro de Lago in No Man's Land, the Tower road landmark in Win-netka, the North Shore Station in Glencoe, and, finally, the gates of Ravinia Park, all ending with a party with prizes at 443 Sheridan Road, Glencoe.

As for the plans for me, I was to remain with the Perlsteins through the school year, and summer, then move back with my parents once they found suitable housing in Chicago. The Perlsteins would continue to fund my schooling and personal expenses after that. I was to visit them at least once a month. I dared not think of what it would do to my relationships with the friends I had on the North Shore, since I could no longer participate in all their social activities, but Aunt Anne made sure when I came to visit, any number of my friends were present. For the time being, everything went on status quo and I doubled my efforts in school activities. I knew the switch to a Chicago high school would be a let down, but again, it would be up to me to make it a positive experience.

November 11, 1937

Dear Daughter Thea,

Today is what you call "Armistice Day", a day when everyone was glad the Great World War was over. For Germany it was a total humiliation, and the beginning of what was to become the Third Reich. Little did we know how far it would extend. I only knew that I and some of my soldier companions were dismissed in Romania, and told to get back to Germany the best we could. We started walking ...

It took us over a year to reach home, a year of depending on the goodness of people, who, only a short time before, had been our enemies. Our families thought we were dead, and it seemed like a miracle when we arrived at the borders of Germany and could inform them otherwise.

I started my life over again then, as I will start over again now. Everything is all on its G-d-directed way. Our papers are in order, as are the all-important entrance visas. I can now write our own sailing tickets. We shall leave here in a week, so this will probably be the last letter I will write you.

It's been a long three years for us. More pain than joy, but for you, thankfully, the other way around. I hope you will not be disappointed in the change in us. Your carefree parents do not exist anymore. We have, however, become more resolute to put the past behind us.

So here we are: ready to ship out on November 18th on the S.S. New York. We should reach New York City about the 28th of November and after a few days in that city, shall be in Chicago in early December.

As much as I try to project, I cannot really picture our reunion. I leave that in the hands of G-d.

Until then ... as we have always been,

Your Devoted Family, Your Dad, Your Pappa

That time in my memory ...

It seems singularly appropriate that this last letter of Pappa's should be dated November 11th, the day that brought peace to the world after the First World War, but, at the same time, laid the social and economic foundations for the Second World War. That date had brought peace to the nations of 1918, and now brought peace to my family, as they began their exodus to a new land and a new life.

It is hard to describe the laughter, the tears, and the embraces that took place at our first meeting. It was the beginning of another phase in my rich, diversified life. The main thing was, we were together again. Of course, my parents had aged and seemed much smaller than I remembered them. Ruth was now the same age I was when I left Germany. Whatever happened now would be in safety and peace.

The nightmare years were over. Still, the thought of those left behind still caused anxiety. One of my aunts and family, by crossing the Rhine to stay with relatives, ended up in a Polish concentration camp and perished. Had they remained in their home in the Palatinate, they would have been interned in France and could have survived. Uncle Herman and his family died in the first fire bombing of Amsterdam. I could have been with them. Who is to say?

I brought Pappa to New Trier, to show him how he had come full circle and he gave Mr. Gaffney, the principal, a replica of the Porta Negra—the symbol of "Old Trier".

I was content.

Thea Kahn—Aged 16

Kahn Family Reunion in Chicago—1940
Left to right: Meier Zissman, Gertrude Lowenstein, Millie Zissman (née Lowenstein),
(Aunt) Lydia Lowenstein (née Samuel), Ernest Lowenstein, Samuel Kahn,
Siegfried Kronfeld (kneeling), Frieda Kahn (née Samuel), Ruth Kahn,
Thea Kahn.
Gerda Kronfeld (née Kahn) took the photo.

Epilogue

My family arrived in the United States in early December 1937 and moved into the hotel where my Uncle Ernest was the maintenance engineer. Our joy at seeing each other cannot be described. Yes, we had all gotten older, Mamma more so than any of the others, but then I had expected that with all she had been through. In exchange for Pappa's services as a bookkeeper and Mamma as a housekeeper, the hotel provided them with a small, one bedroom apartment. There they stayed until something was made available to them when Pappa found a more suitable job in the merchandising field. Eventually they moved into a small apartment in a quiet neighborhood of Chicago.

I still continued living with the Perlsteins until the following fall when I joined my family in Chicago. That summer was my 16th birthday, and it was celebrated in grand style. Aunt Anne and Uncle Harry invited six of my best friends to an overnight party at the Edgewater Beach Hotel. It was a wonderful passage into young womanhood, and we were all aware of the changes in our lives. Much as we pledged to always stay in touch with each other, the inevitable would happen ... the parting of interests, and eventual estrangement. It all left us a little sad, but looking to a great future with all sorts of successful careers.

My generous allowance from the Perlsteins helped with the Kahn family finances. Pappa would not accept any financial help otherwise.

I graduated from Lake View High School in Chicago, where I still maintained a 4.0 grade point average, was a member of the National Honor Society, and was active in the Drama and Art Departments. Upon graduation, I attended the Chicago Academy of Fine Arts with a commercial art career in mind. I also took courses in creative writing at Northwestern University. Sad to say, a full enrollment at that excellent school was not possible—the art courses there were not along the lines of commercial art, which was a concern. I needed to be gainfully employed as soon as possible. Two years was all I could spare for that training.

When I left the North Shore, my social life out there declined, which is understandable. What mattered was that we were a united family once again.

Pappa's job situation continued to improve. After several attempts as a salesman, he became Merchandise Shipping Manager for a lingerie manufacturer—a job that was secure enough for Mamma to leave her position at the hotel.

Ruth thrived at school. My parents became active members of the German Jewish refugee community, and Pappa got an additional job as the Cantor at the newly founded Temple Ezra.

My adjustment was more difficult, as I felt that I was living two lives. My former life was receding fast. I found new American friends, but had only limited contact with the German community, since their activities were centered about European traditions, and I had become far removed from that.

Upon completion of my art school education, I joined the Chicago commercial arts community as a designer and layout artist for several Chicago studios, with the option of working in New York intermittently. I felt my life was very complete. At the beginning of World War II, I returned to Chicago and once more lived near my parents, who had moved into a large, airy apartment on Chicago's North Side.

And what of the Jews left in Germany?

The passage of more and more restrictive measures against the Jews continued unabated after 1937. My family was extremely fortunate to have left Germany when they did, for the anti-Semitic measures enacted in Germany in 1938 dwarfed everything that preceded them. In August 1938, new laws announced that henceforth all Jewish men would have to adopt the name "Israel" and all Jewish women the name "Sarah." Furthermore their passports would be marked with the letter "J." But worse was to come.

In early November 1938 the Nazis seized upon the excuse of the assassination of a Nazi envoy in Paris by a Polish Jew to unleash the most massive and public demonstration of anti-Semitism since the Russian pogroms of thirty years earlier. During the night of 9-10 November, synagogues and Jewish businesses all over Germany were ransacked and demolished by Nazi gangs abetted by the S.A. and the police. This was "Kristalnacht", an ironic and insulting name that mocked all of the broken glass from Jewish store windows which looked like crystal on the streets of German cities.

Over 1600 synagogues were destroyed or badly damaged, and as a further insult, Hitler blamed the violence on the Jews themselves and levied a fine of one billion Reichsmarks against the collective Jewish population. When it was discovered that many of the Jewish businesses were insured, and that to indemnify the owners would bankrupt the German insurance industry, Hitler calmly suspended all payments to such would-be recipients and declared that the Jews themselves would be held responsible for making good on their own damages!

The start of World War II removed any vestigial constraints on Hitler's handling of the Jews. They were sent to various camps either in Germany or other occupied countries to be worked and exploited until they died.

By January 1942 his burgeoning empire had absorbed more than a dozen countries—and their Jewish populations to boot. That month Nazi leaders sat down at a villa at Wannsee in Berlin to lay out the "Final Solution" to the Jewish Problem. The solution—no matter what they called it or how they mitigated its brutality—was utter extermination of the Jews of Europe.

Thus, out a thriving population of more than a half a million German Jews in 1933, no more than 15,000 were able to survive in Germany: All the rest either emigrated or were exterminated.

But my family—father, mother, and all four daughters safely living in Chicago, California, and Brazil—prevailed and survived.

At the end of the War, then, I met Lieutenant Harry Lindauer, freshly returned from the battlegrounds of Europe, and ready to resume civilian life and complete his college education. His background was the same as mine—his family had also escaped the European Holocaust. We were totally compatible and married in 1946.

Wedding picture of Thea Kahn and 1LT Harry Lindauer, US Army
Reserve, 27 Oct. 1946

Since Harry was still in the U.S. Army Reserve, he was recalled for service during the Korean War. We now had a young son, but I continued my free-lance artist's career. After the birth of a daughter, Marian Joan, I joined my husband in Japan, where, again, I resumed the study of art.

Upon our return to the States, he made the decision to remain in the Armed Forces, where the career opportunities for worldwide assignments as interpreters were excellent. We had another daughter, Robin Carol.

And so we continued …

Tours in Germany provided exciting involvement for both of us at high government levels in our former homeland. Speaking the language, we were very much in the foreground of liaison activities, particularly those that involved the reconciliation of former German Jews with the new Germany. It earned my husband the highest honor paid a German or foreign national, das Grosse Verdienst Kreuz (the equivalent of a Medal of Honor). Still very much in pursuit of an art career, I had the opportunity to connect with some of the erstwhile innovators of what had been the German Modern Art Movement.

After our final European assignment, we returned to the USA where I settled in Annapolis, Maryland. By now, Colonel Lindauer was due for a tour of duty in Vietnam, and left me and two of the three children in Annapolis, while the oldest attended college.

There, I was really able to build on my love of the Arts in a three-pronged direction: music, painting, and writing. All of my projects are too numerous to list, but a few of them ranged from designing a new chapel at the U.S. Naval Academy, to running the emerging Annapolis Opera Company, being a member of the Board and designing publicity for the Annapolis Symphony Orchestra, translating German naval books into English for the Naval Institute, and teaching a course in Design for the Seniors' Program of Anne Arundel Community College. All of this kept me very involved with the success of the Arts in Annapolis and Anne Arundel County, Maryland.

As a result I was honored to become one of the "100 Influential Women in the State of Maryland" in the year 1998.

The Perlstein family, as I knew them, no longer exists. Anne Perlstein died many years ago, followed by Betty Ann, who had married Kenneth Cowan and had two daughters. Uncle Harry had retired and moved to the Gold Coast of Chicago with his second wife. We celebrated his 80th birthday at the Drake Hotel with Jimmy Durante holding forth with the non-stop entertainment. Uncle Harry died in 1986 at the age of 93, one day before his 94th birthday. Larry died in the latter part of 1990—we had not been in touch since the birthday party. I believe he had four children.

And as for me ...

AS ONE OF THE THOUSAND CHILDREN, INC ...

I married a fellow refugee, one of General George S. Patton's "sassy young lieutenants", a career officer who rose to the rank of Colonel in the U.S. Army, and after the war was presented with a high German honor for his efforts in the reconciliation between Germany and its former Jewish citizens.

AS ONE OF THE THOUSAND CHILDREN, INC ...

I raised a son, David, who received an Army ROTC Scholarship to Georgetown University's School of Foreign Service, became an Army paratrooper, and now works as a Washington D.C. contractor overseeing defense plans and budgets. He has two sons, Charles and Michael.

AS ONE OF THE THOUSAND CHILDREN, INC ...

I raised a daughter, Marian Joan, who married Bill Gregory, a US Naval Academy graduate, and had three daughters. The oldest, Kristin Gregory Honeycutt, is an elementary school teacher. The middle daughter, Leslie Gregory Vojta, graduated from USNA thirty years after her father and was selected as to participate in the Uniformed Services University for the Health Services Medical School in Bethesda, MD. She is currently on active duty with the U.S. Air Force, along with her husband, Capt Chris Vojta. The youngest daughter, Sarah Gregory is also a Midshipman at the U.S. Naval Academy.

AS ONE OF THE THOUSAND CHILDREN, INC ...

I raised another daughter, Robin, an occupational therapist who was married to Timothy Lang in the small interfaith chapel that I designed and helped establish at the US Naval Academy. She explains the rituals of the Jewish Holidays at her three children's Catholic Parochial School. Her children Rebecca, Katherine, and Theresa, are still in school, the first two in college, and the youngest in middle school.

AS ONE OF THE THOUSAND CHILDREN, INC ...

I was selected as one of the 100 Women of Achievement in Maryland for their contribution to the Arts in the year 1998.

AS ONE OF THE THOUSAND CHILDREN, INC ...

I received the Anne Arundel County, Maryland 2006 "Life Achievement in the Arts" award.

JUST ONE OF THE THOUSAND CHILDREN, INC.

Author's Note

In 2001 a British film won the Oscar in the Best Documentary Category in that year's judging competition. "Into The Arms of Strangers" was the story of 10,000 children's escape from the engulfing holocaust of Hitler's Europe and who were brought to England. Some of their stories, their trials and tribulations—even after they were saved—bear somber witness to the heartbreak suffered by many families—tragedies that took place over and over again at that time.

In my great curiosity I remembered an earlier time, 1934 to be exact, when a similar attempt was made to bring children from Germany to the United States for "an experiment in education:" A rescue by people who foresaw a threatening future. What happened to those children? Where and how did those children survive?

With that question in mind, and since I was one of them, I contacted TIME, NEWSWEEK, and the WASHINGTON POST to make them aware of the 1934 experiment exodus.

My letter was duly published in all the periodicals, but it was the WASHINGTON POST that put me in touch with the directors of a newly formed research committee headed by Iris Posner and Lenore Muskowitz. They explained that the mission of the committee was to find out what happened to these children.

At the same time, a study called "The Second Wave" was initiated at Harvard under Professor Gerhardt Sonnert, a German historian with the same goal in mind.

So far their research had uncovered 1000 children that came out of Europe in driblets over the years 1934—1945. At the very beginning the program had little support. It was considered a futile attempt, since very few parents saw a cataclysmic threat to their children's future. Second, no parents in their right mind (see the description of my father in the Prologue) would send a young child across an ocean to be raised by an unknown family. Third, the "profile" of the eligible children was sketchy and difficult to picture in its concept. This was the dilemma faced by "Hebrew Immigrant Aid Society" (HIAS) and the lawmakers in Congress in their worthy attempts.

In meetings with Posner and Professor Sonnert I became aware of how different my upbringing was from the usual Holocaust victims—a Holocaust survivor nevertheless.

While moving into a retirement community I miraculously discovered my father's original letters to me, letters written during the period when I left Germany until my parents arrived in the United States over three years later.

I translated these letters for a symposium with the Directors of "The 1000 Children Inc." in Chicago in the summer of 2002. Translating these letters was no problem as I had been doing translations of German literature purchased by the Naval Institute.

Dr. Larry Thompson, Head of the History Department, U.S. Naval Academy, suggested that I should "flesh them out" into a full blown manuscript, recall all that occurred to me at the time each letter was written, and the events that shaped my life at that time.

Remembering back 70 years was quite a task, traumatic in retrospect, but for the most part still alive in my mind.

Sad to say, many of the people who figured prominently in my growing up are no longer alive and able to enrich my memory. Their gifts will always be with me.

978-0-595-45240-8
0-595-45240-X

Printed in the United States
97313LV00003B/1-108/A

9 780595 452408